The Shape of Sacred Space

American Academy of Religion
Studies in Religion
edited by

James O. Duke

Number 23
The Shape of Sacred Space
Four Biblical Studies
by Robert L. Cohn

The Shape of Sacred Space
Four Biblical Studies

Robert L. Cohn

Scholars Press

BS
630
.C57

Distributed by
Scholars Press
101 Salem Street
PO Box 2268
Chico, California 95927

The Shape of Sacred Space:
Four Biblical Studies

by
Robert L. Cohn

Library of Congress Cataloging in Publication Data

Cohn, Robert L
    The shape of sacred space.
    (Studies in religion ; no. 23 ISSN 0084-6287)
    Includes bibliographical references.
    1. Bible. O.T.–Geography–Addresses, essays,
lectures. 2. Bible. O.T.–History of Biblical
events–Addresses, essays, lectures. I. Title. II. Series:
American Academy of Religion. AAR studies in
religion ; no. 23.

BS630.C57   221.'9'1   80-11086
ISBN 0-89130-384-7

Printed in the United States of America
1 2 3 4 5
Edwards Brothers, Inc.
Ann Arbor, MI. 48104

For my parents,
Matilda and Harold Cohn

CONTENTS

1. INTRODUCTION 1
2. LIMINALITY IN THE WILDERNESS 7
3. MOUNTAINS IN THE BIBLICAL COSMOS 25
4. THE SINAI SYMBOL 43
5. THE SENSES OF A CENTER 63

Chapter One

INTRODUCTION

Thanks largely to the creative work of Mircea Eliade, sacred time and sacred space are now common categories used in the comparative study of religions. In biblical studies, however, attention has long focused on time rather than space. Because interpreters have generally distinguished Yahweh from other gods as a God who acts in history, they have stressed Israel's memory of those moments in which Yahweh intervened to save or punish his people. Israel's self-consciousness about the "mighty acts of Yahweh," remembered in song and story and celebrated in the cult, set this people apart from the surrounding cultures. For those cultures, according to the still regnant view, time moved cyclically rather than linearly, and sacred times were eternal repetitions of primal events or celebrations of nature's annual cycle.

Not only has the dimension of space been neglected, but this view of time itself must be modified. Bertil Albrektson has argued convincingly that other ancient Near Eastern gods also intervened purposefully in history; they were not only or primarily nature gods.[1] Furthermore, although Israel's sacred times often recalled historical events, these events were mythicized in their recollection, so that they too became loosened from their historical moorings. Still, when the theme has been thoroughly nuanced, it remains true that for Israel, history, conceived as a purposeful sequence of divine-human encounters, served as the organizing principle for communicating the Israelite experience of Yahweh in the Hebrew Bible.

Of course, Israel experienced Yahweh in space as well as in time. In fact, unlike most ancient gods, Yahweh moved from place to place with his people: guiding Abraham in the promised land, liberating the Hebrews from Egypt, wandering with Israel in the wilderness, dwelling with David in Jerusalem, accompanying Judahites to Babylonian exile. The Bible evinces a deep meditation on the space with which Yahweh is associated. The land of Israel is always Yahweh's land; it belongs to Israel not by right but by promise. It is "the land which the Lord your God cares for" (Deut. 11–12); not conquest but Yahweh's favor establishes Israel's hold on the land. Its topography, climate, agriculture,

---

[1] Bertil Albrektson, *History and the Gods* (Lund, Sweden: CWK Gleerup, 1967), esp. pp. 11–41.

and, especially, its role in the divine purpose are causes for wonder and awe. Furthermore, the land of Israel is radically distinct from other lands. They are alien places, places to be delivered *from*. Abraham first forsakes Haran and forbids his servant from letting Isaac return there (Gen. 24:6). Yahweh then liberates the Hebrews from Egypt and forbids them to go back (Exod. 14:13; cf. Isa. 31:1). Mesopotamia and Egypt, the great civilizations of the ancient Near East, were off limits because they were not Yahweh's lands. Indeed, the Babylonian exiles lamented their inability to "sing the Lord's song in a foreign land" (Ps. 137:4), while their fellow refugees in Egypt had abducted Jeremiah apparently to assure access to the word of the Lord (Jer. 43:5–7). Salvation is being within Yahweh's land; exile is always catastrophe.

Israel's spatial sensitivity would thus seem to be a crucial dimension in a comparative approach to the biblical tradition. I cannot agree with Hans-J. Klimkeit that Israel "has its special position on account of the great *historical* deeds of Yahweh, not on account of its *geographical* environment, or the geographical factors of its *Lebensraum*" (author's emphasis).[2] On the contrary, even the "historical deeds of Yahweh" themselves involve intimately Israel's geographical environment: the promise of, delivery to, settlement in, and exile from the land of Canaan. As Walter Brueggemann puts it,

> Land is a central, if not the *central theme* of biblical faith . . . . It will no longer do to talk about Yahweh and his people but we must speak about Yahweh and his people *and his land.* Preoccupation with existentialist *decisions* and transforming *events* has distracted us from seeing that this God is committed to this land and that his promise for his people is always his land [author's emphasis].[3]

Moreover, the Bible's "sacred geography," its variety of religious *topoi* and *temenoi*, presents a complex picture of the geographical foci of Israelite religion. How they were conceived, how they functioned, and how both conception and function changed over time are important topics for biblical studies.

Contemporary concerns, interestingly, have conspired to underscore the relevance of the investigation of biblical spatial thinking. First of all, more and more scholars are spending time in the land of Israel digging and climbing. This physical contact with the land has raised a generation's consciousness about the importance of the *realia* of the land for understanding biblical thought. Then, too, the perdurance of the state of Israel has prompted reflection among both Jewish and Christian scholars on the theological significance of the land and the state. Two

---

[2] Hans-J. Klimkeit, "Spatial Orientation in Mythical Thinking as Exemplified in Ancient Egypt: Considerations Toward a Geography of Religions," *History of Religions* 14 (1975):269.

[3] Walter Brueggemann, *The Land* (Philadelphia: Fortress, 1977), p. 3.

diasporic faith communities have had to cope differently with the religious dimensions of a particular land in which both are rooted. Finally, in a more general way, ecological issues have focused attention on the space in which we live. While, obviously, our environment affects our physical health, it also conditions our mental, and even spiritual attitudes. Thus, the current social atmosphere provides a natural setting for the study of the religious meaning of geographical phenomena.

I offer these essays as contributions to that general study. Each explores the religious meaning of an important element of biblical geography. The first two focus on broad spatial areas: the wilderness and the mountains. In the realm of space, the wilderness, first of all, occupies an anomalous position in biblical life. It is neither within the promised land nor within the sphere of "the nations." In the south the wilderness forms a buffer zone between Israel and Egypt, and in the east, between Israel and Mesopotamia. As such, the wilderness is a no-man's land, on the periphery of civilization. This unique status helps explain the use of the wilderness motif in the story of Israel's forty-year trial period following the "exodus" from Egypt. The first essay, "Liminality in the Wilderness," interprets the story of the wilderness journey as a narrative paradigm of a "liminal" (threshold) time and space. The priestly author-compilers found in this story a vehicle through which to express their own liminal experience of Babylonian exile. This essay applies and tests the usefulness of a model developed by the social anthropologist Victor Turner for studying rites and symbols of transition.

The second essay shifts the stage from the periphery to the land itself. The land of Canaan possessed neither an irrigated river valley, as did Egypt and Mesopotamia, nor a great fertile plain. Israel occupied Canaan's hill country, where permanent settlement had only recently been made possible by the invention of iron tools for clearing forests and plastered cisterns for storing water. This hilly environment undoubtedly stands behind the rich use of mountain imagery in biblical literature. "The Mountains in the Biblical Cosmos" analyzes the mountain motif and shows how it is concentrated and reapplied in the poetic description of the monarchy's foremost sacred place, Mount Zion-Jerusalem.

The last two essays explore the symbolic functions of the Bible's two most important sacred places: Mount Sinai in the midst of the wilderness and Jerusalem in the center of the hill country. The movement from Sinai to Zion neatly encapsulates geographically the flow of biblical sacred history from the Pentateuch through the Prophets. "The Sinai Symbol" examines the imagery of theophany and instruction associated with this mountain and synthesizes its symbolic valences in the biblical tradition. Although already during the monarchy Mount Sinai had apparently ceased to function as an active *hieros topos*, it did live on in memory and legend. Its symbolic role, in fact, set it into a direct and sometimes rival relationship with Mount Zion in later literature. The final essay, "The Senses of a Center," contends that changing political and social conditions from biblical through early rabbinic times conditioned the ways in which Jerusalem was symbolized as a "center." Like the first essay, it is programmatic in nature: it applies and nuances the theory of Mircea Eliade. I demonstrate that "symbolism of the center" is dependent less on a universal archetype than on a culture's concrete historical circumstances. Together the four essays thus span the length of biblical sacred history and the "width" of its sacred geography.

These essays were written over several years' time, but they share some common methodological approaches which should be made explicit. First, I am little concerned here with the origin and development of the biblical text or with the history of traditions. I am most interested, rather, in the "biblical imagination," that collection of perspectives which the compiled, edited, and canonized text mediates. To be sure, the Bible preserves only those interpretations of the life of ancient Israel which the early Jewish community found meaningful; yet these interpretations represent crucial dimensions of the Israelite religious mind. The motifs traced in these essays thus cut across the layers of literature which critical scholarship has identified. For the study of religious symbolism the final text is, indeed, the most important, for it contains the richest deposit of tradition. At the same time, I point to issues which have engaged critical biblical scholarship.

Second, as I do not focus on the history of the text or the history of traditions, so, too, I do not trace in detail the history of the motifs or symbols prior to and outside of their employment in the Bible. Biblical writers certainly "borrowed" literary formulas, images, and symbols from the surrounding ancient Near Eastern cultures and "translated" them into biblical language. Thus the imagery of the Sinai theophany owes much to Canaanite descriptions of Baal and El. My purpose here, however, is to examine how the wilderness and mountain motifs and the Sinai and Zion symbols function in the *biblical* imagination. Their foreign origins and relations are not directly relevant to this purpose.

Third, I deal with these biblical symbols in the historical and geographical reality of Israelite-Jewish culture. Comparative studies often work with universal archetypes which tend to be quite abstract. Categories such as "wilderness" or "center" ought not to be imposed on apparently amenable data without careful study of the data on its own terms. Although Sinai and Zion are both "sacred mountains," for instance, they function quite differently in the biblical imagination. Thus, by stressing the particular concrete circumstances in which the religious mind functioned, I intend to show how symbols reflect cultural particularity.

This work, nonetheless, represents a meeting between biblical studies and the history of religions. Although I make no comparisons across traditions, comparative concerns inform all of the essays. Mounts Sinai and Zion, for instance, are compared as religious symbols. In addition, the first and last essays are explicitly applications of history of religions methodology.

These four essays, then, are intended primarily for students of religion with a comparative bent. They provide a pathway through biblical sacred history by tracing some aspects of its geographical imagery and symbolism. The first and last may be of special use in undergraduate settings as illustrations of the application to biblical materials of important comparative theory. Essays two and three integrate literary imagery not usually so treated and, thus, should interest students of literature as well.

I am grateful for the support which I received from the Department of Religious Studies at The Pennsylvania State University, where I wrote the essays, and from the Department of History and Literature of Religions at Northwestern University, my present home, where I revised them. Also, the editors of *Judaism* and the *Journal of the American Academy of Religion* have kindly permitted me to revise and include here two essays which first appeared in those journals.

I am especially indebted to several people for their criticism and encouragement: Denise Carmody, John Carmody, Conrad Cherry, Edwin Good, Shemaryahu Talmon, Judith van Herik, and my good wife, Renée.

Chapter Two

LIMINALITY IN THE WILDERNESS

Of all the periods in the history of ancient Israel none is more intractable to the modern historian than the wilderness period, the traditional forty years that elapsed between the departure from Egypt and the entry into Canaan. Although much of the Pentateuch is devoted to a description of the journey through the wilderness, the narrative yields little historical data about the journey. John Bright succinctly states the dilemma facing the historian.

> We cannot undertake to reconstruct the details of Israel's wanderings in the desert, both because the actual events were doubtless vastly more complex than the biblical narrative indicates, and because almost none of the places mentioned can be identified with any certainty. But that it was during this period that Israel received her distinctive faith and became a people can scarcely be doubted.[1]

But if the narrative is nearly opaque to the historical wilderness period, as sacred history it reveals the perspective on that period of successive generations of Israelites. In particular, the final shape of the Pentateuch was most likely the work of exilic writers. These "priestly" authors compiled, supplemented, edited, and ordered the old epic tradition, and they or their successors appended the book of Deuteronomy as a fitting hortatory conclusion.[2] The exilic writers preserved and reworked the wilderness tradition, especially, because it provided a paradigm with which to understand their own experience.

> In the priests' narrative the chosen people are last seen as pilgrims moving through alien land toward a goal to be fulfilled in another time and place, and this is the vision, drawn from the ancient story of their past, that the priests now hold out to the scattered sons and daughters of old Israel.[3]

---

[1] John Bright, *A History of Israel*, 2d ed. (Philadelphia: Westminster, 1975), p. 122.

[2] For a clear discussion of basic source-critical theory see H. H. Rowley, *The Growth of the Old Testament* (New York: Harper, 1963), pp. 25–37. For a recent summary of scholarship on P, the "priestly source," see B. A. Levine, "Priestly Writers," *The Interpreter's Dictionary of the Bible, Supplementary Volume* (Nashville: Abingdon, 1976), pp. 683–87.

[3] W. Lee Humphreys, *Crisis and Story: Introduction to the Old Testament* (Palo Alto: Mayfield, 1979), p. 217.

Into the story of the wilderness march, the exiles projected their own fears and hopes. Like generations before them, they viewed the wilderness as a chaotic place and the march as a terrifying journey, yet as the space-time coordinates in which a new community was created out of the chaos of despair. They thus saw themselves in the "wilderness" of exile being purged of the old and primed for the new. Similarly, the exiles at Qumran, several centuries later, understood themselves to be the wilderness generation *redivivus* and read their own story out of the Pentateuchal account.[4]

It must be admitted that nowhere in the Pentateuch is the place of the exile specifically called "wilderness." Of course even the possibility of exile is discussed only twice there (Lev. 26; Deut. 28). Yet the image of exile in other literature of the age strengthens the claim that the exiles saw themselves in a "wilderness." The author of Jeremiah's "Book of Consolation," for instance, promises that God's love for Israel persists even after the destruction of Jerusalem. "The people who survived the sword found grace in the wilderness" (31:2). Here exile is specifically wilderness, refuge from war, until the Lord rebuilds the virgin Israel (v. 4). In Ezekiel's vision of the new Israel the return to the land is accompanied by land distribution, the bequeathing of the *naḥalāh*, "inheritance," modeled on the distribution in Joshua.[5] By implication, then, the exiles are homologous with Joshua's compatriots, the generation of the wilderness.

A more common image, however, is the return from exile as a new exodus (e.g., Jer. 16:14f.; 23:7f.; Isa. 43:16–19). Here Egypt, rather than wilderness, is the metaphor for exile. Yet this image was eventually found wanting theologically, for although exile was the result of sin, Egyptian enslavement was never so viewed.[6] Thus, in Nehemiah 9 restoration is not a new exodus, as in Jeremiah, but only another act of God's mercy. Interestingly, here in Ezra's great confession, wilderness and exile are paralleled: "Thou in thy great mercies did not forsake them in the wilderness . . . . Nevertheless in thy great mercies thou didst not make an end of them or forsake them [in exile]" (Neh. 9:19,31). Only with reference to these two periods—wilderness and exile—is the phrase "not forsake them" used. For Ezra, the experience of exile was the passport to membership in the restored community. Exile, like wilderness, was seen to be the arena of both judgment and promise. Those who joined Ezra's covenant community, like those who joined Joshua's (Josh. 24), had to affirm their passage through the "wilderness."

---

[4] See S. Talmon's discussion of this phenomenon in "The 'Desert Motif' in the Bible and in Qumran Literature," *Biblical Motifs: Origins and Transformations*, ed. A. Altmann (Cambridge, Mass.: Harvard University Press, 1966), pp. 55–63.

[5] Brueggemann, *The Land*, pp. 142–43.

[6] Peter R. Ackroyd, *Exile and Restoration* (Philadelphia: Westminster, 1968), p. 238.

All three groups—the wilderness generation, the Babylonian exiles, the Qumranians—were or saw themselves to be societies in transition, not settled in time or space, but on the move and awaiting the fulfillment of divine promises. The wilderness narrative in the Pentateuch depicts a people in transition between slavery in Egypt and freedom in Canaan. The way in which the narrative functioned paradigmatically for Israel is highlighted when its preoccupations are seen in comparative context against the background of those of other transitional groups.

In this task the work of Victor Turner provides a rich basis for analysis. Turner has studied the symbols and behaviors manifested in a wide variety of social and religious phenomena of transition such as rites of passage, millenarian movements, and pilgrimages. The theory he develops seems useful as an interpretive tool for understanding the wilderness narrative and, perhaps, for revealing the conditions of the wilderness period itself.[7] This essay is concerned to interpret the wilderness narrative with Turner's categories and to assess their usefulness. In the process both the typical and the singular features of the biblical description should come into sharper focus. First, we discuss those aspects of Turner's theoretical work which are relevant to the narrative at hand. Next, we extend this theory to the narrative and identify those features of the narrative which the theory highlights. Finally, we move from the literary to the historical level and suggest the implications of this interpretation for understanding the social process in Israel.

Liminality and Communitas

Victor Turner's work on phenomena of transition began with his study of rites of passage which he observed extensively among the Ndembu of Zambia. Following Arnold van Gennep, Turner identifies three phases in these rites: (1) separation of the ritual subject from his role in the social structure; (2) margin or *limen*, the transition stage; (3) reincorporation of the subject into his new role in society.[8] In the second or transition phase, particularly emphasized in initiation rites, Turner finds a variety of behaviors and symbols which provide a key to understanding the ritual process and a clue to the dynamics of social process.

---

[7] Of the many books and articles which Victor Turner has written, I have relied in this essay on the following: *The Ritual Process: Structure and Anti-Structure* (Chicago: Aldin, 1969); *Dramas, Fields, and Metaphors* (Ithaca, N.Y.: Cornell University Press, 1974); "Liminal to Liminoid, in Play, Flow, and Ritual," *Rice University Studies* (1974), pp.53–92; Victor Turner and Edith Turner, *Image and Pilgrimage in Christian Culture: Anthropological Perspectives* (New York: Columbia University Press, 1978).

[8] Turner, *The Ritual Process*, p. 94. See Arnold van Gennep, *The Rites of Passage* (Chicago: University of Chicago Press, 1960), esp. pp. 15–25.

In the liminal phase the ritual subject is "betwixt and between" the position assigned by law, custom, convention, and ceremonial.[9] He has undergone a symbolic death to his old life and is in process of being reborn to a new one. His situation in the ritual is often likened in the lore to being in the womb or the wilderness, to invisibility, to darkness, to an eclipse of the sun or moon, to bisexuality. He is sexless or androgynous. He is out of time and space, a threshold being. Liminality is "a sphere or domain of action or thought" described by certain metaphors that span religious frontiers.[10]

Turner introduces the term "communitas" to identify the nature of social relationships among liminal subjects. "Communitas" is a type of bonding which, unlike the dominant mode of human relationship in society, does not depend on class, rank, wealth, or social status. In contrast to structured, premeditated, status-bound human interaction, the bonds of communitas are "undifferentiated, egalitarian, direct, extant, non-rational, existential, I-Thou."[11] Comradeship among liminars is spontaneous, immediate, concrete, potentially universal and boundless, not shaped by the customs, laws, and norms of social structure. Submitting to the authority of the ritual elders, the subjects experience the equality of sharing a common predicament. Thus, the modes of acting and thinking (liminality) and relating (communitas) of ritual subjects during rites of passage are different from those of people in fixed social positions.

Liminality and the communitas it engenders, moreover, have social and religious manifestations broader than rites of passage. For instance, "enthusiastic" or millenarian movements may be called liminal because they arise during periods in which societies are undergoing radical structural shifts. The qualities of such movements correspond closely to those of rites of passage: homogeneity, equality, anonymity, absence of property, uniform apparel, sexual continence (or its antithesis, sexual community), abolition of rank, unselfishness, and others.[12] The "revolution" sets itself against society's structure; it is free, open, and unbounded, unrestricted to a particular ethnic or social group. Of course, in time such movements lose their spontaneity and openness, their communitas, and become institutions with "structure" of their own. Yet initially they are phenomena of transition in which "much of what has been bound by social structure is liberated."[13]

---

[9]Turner, *The Ritual Process*, p. 95.

[10]Turner, *Dramas*, p. 52.

[11] Ibid., p. 274.

[12] Turner, *The Ritual Process*, p. 111.

[13] Turner, *Image and Pilgrimage*, p. 249.

In his most recent work Turner has studied the pilgrimage as a type of social process.[14] He finds that for the "historical" religions, pilgrimages perform a function analogous to that of initiation rites in pre-industrial societies.[15]

> A pilgrim is an initiand, entering into a new, deeper level of existence than he has known in his accustomed milieu. Homologous with the ordeals of tribal initiation are the trials, tribulations, and even temptations of the pilgrim's way. And at the end the pilgrim, like the novice, is exposed to powerful religious sacra . . . the beneficial effect of which depends upon the zeal and pertinacity of his quest.[16]

The pilgrim leaves the familiar for the far, leaves society and joins for a time an egalitarian community on a liminal journey toward a sacred place. The pilgrimage is the "quintessence of voluntary liminality" through which the historical religions provide an organized outlet for communitas.[17] The holy journey can be penitential, cleansing, transformative. The pilgrim reenters society as a new person, ensouled with the breath of communitas.

Liminality and communitas together define "anti-structure," one of the two modes in which society sees itself. Society, for Turner, is either a "differentiated, segmented system of structural positions" [structure] or a "homogeneous undifferentiated whole" [anti-structure].[18] The values of communitas treasured by liminal groups in the niches and interstices of society lead Turner to suggest that regular doses of communitas are necessary to keep a social group healthy.

> The basic and perennial human social problem is to discover what is the right relation between these modalities [anti-structure and structure] at a specific time and place . . . . The great historical religions have, in the course of time, learned how to incorporate enclaves of communitas within their institutionalized structures . . . .[19]

Thus, Turner, while beginning modestly enough by describing ritual behavior among African tribes, develops a theory for understanding social process in general. He focuses his attention not on fixed social states but on change, on the "processual view of society." "The social world is a world in becoming, not a world in being (except insofar as 'being' is a description of the static, atemporal models men have in

---

[14] Turner's first article on the pilgrimage process, "The Center Out There: Pilgrim's Goal," *History of Religions* 12 (1973):191–230, became the chapter "Pilgrimages and Social Processes" in *Dramas*. His latest book, *Image and Pilgrimage*, is a rich study of several modern Christian pilgrimages.

[15] Turner, *Dramas*, p. 182.

[16] Turner, *Image and Pilgrimage*, p. 8.

[17] Ibid., p. 9.

[18] Turner, *Dramas*, pp. 237–38.

[19] Ibid., pp. 266–67.

their heads), and for this reason studies of social structure *as such* are irrelevant."[20] Through his illuminating discussions of the thought and actions of liminars, Turner draws our attention to the similar preoccupations of different kinds of "threshold beings." By unpacking the symbols that appear in the rituals and literature of these groups, he reveals a common language through which the values of communitas are expressed. Any theory which attempts to explain such a diverse group of phenomena, however, runs the risk of being so general that it explains little. Furthermore, the heavy use of jargon can obscure rather than clarify. Nonetheless, despite these potential dangers, Turner's theory seems genuinely illuminating. We next shall see what light it sheds on the biblical materials.

The Wilderness Narrative

Two notes are in order at the outset about the nature of the materials and the approach. First, for the social anthropologist, the materials present a problem. There is no field work to be done, no new data to gather, no eyewitness reporting. All of the data is in the Hebrew Bible, and it was written, collected, compiled, and redacted over the course of many centuries. When we deal with the wilderness narrative, we are treating a literary composition that bears little direct relationship to the time period it purports to describe. This means that we must deal primarily with the way in which the narrative depicts its subject, not with the historical subject itself. Therefore, we will here discuss the wilderness narrative, not the actual wilderness period, and will reflect historically only in the final section.

At the same time, because the approach is, broadly speaking, comparative, we will not engage in source-critical, form-critical, or history of traditions analysis. We are concerned with the wilderness narrative only in its final form. The canonical Pentateuch represents the most complete development of ancient Israel's wilderness traditions and thus, as it stands, is the richest source for understanding their paradigmatic function. We thus consider as data all of the literature connected by the "wilderness itinerary" (Exod. 12:37–Num. 25:18) and the book of Deuteronomy which is set on the edge of the wilderness.[21] This literature includes Israel's travels and trials in the wilderness, the Sinai theophany and covenant, and the legal corpora. Rather than peel off layers of tradition, we will take the tradition as its stands.

When viewed as a whole, the Pentateuchal picture of Israel in the wilderness is analogous to several of the phenomena which Turner

[20] Ibid., p. 24.
[21] See George Coats, "The Wilderness Itinerary," *Catholic Biblical Quarterly* 34 (1972): 135–52.

describes. Like the initiates in a rite of passage, for instance, the Israelites pass through three distinct phases: (1) separation, the exodus from Egypt in which the crossing of the Red Sea marks the final break ("For the Egyptians whom you see today, you shall never see again" [Exod. 14:13]); (2) *limen*, the transitional period of wandering for forty years; (3) reincorporation, the crossing of the Jordan river, conquest, and settlement in the new land. Like participants on a pilgrimage, they journey to a sacred mountain where a theophany bonds them in a new way. Like the masses of a millenarian or revitalistic movement, they submit to the leadership of a prophet with the plans for a new and open society opposed to the closed hierarchial society of Egypt. Israel thus undergoes a corporate rite of passage, makes a pilgrimage to a sacred mountain, and emerges as an "enthusiastic" socio-religious movement. But beyond these general parallels, the specific emphases of the narrative correspond to the conditions of liminality. These emphases, which we shall now examine, are the wilderness setting, the trial episodes, and the covenant ethic.

Wilderness, first of all, is a typical metaphor for the liminal phase of rites of passage. Participants in initiation rituals are often actually or metaphorically in the wilderness, secluded from society.[22] In the Pentateuch, however, wilderness is not only a metaphor but a geographical reality. Surely at least some of the people who became "Israel" fled through the Sinai desert from Egypt to Canaan.[23] That the authors of the Pentateuch devote so much attention to the narration of the episodes in the wilderness, however, indicates that the significance of the wilderness for them transcends its geophysical existence.

The Hebrew *midbār*, "wilderness," and related wilderness terminology are not simply neutral geographical designations but occur with generally negative connotations in the Bible. Whether it designates agriculturally untapped areas, the drift between the desert and the sown, or the dry zones beyond settled life, *midbār* is the periphery, the undomesticated, the uncivilized, the *'ereṣ lo' zĕrû'āh*, "land unsown" (Jer. 2:2). It is the dwelling place of wild and demonic creatures (Isa. 13:21; 34:14) and the refuge of outlaws and fugitives (Gen. 21:20).[24] The Pentateuchal narrative views the wilderness in light of these negative connotations. It is "that great and terrible wilderness" (Deut. 1:19) to which the fugitive Hebrews flee. There they encounter hunger and thirst, snakes and scorpions, and fierce desert nomads. The difficulty of life in the wilderness is repeatedly contrasted with the security

---

[22] Examples of seclusion of initiands are found in Van Gennep, *The Rites of Passage*, pp. 65–115, and Turner, *Dramas*, pp. 238–39.

[23] See Bright's judicious discussion of this point, *A History of Israel*, pp. 133–39.

[24] This evaluation of biblical *midbār* is taken from S. Talmon's "The 'Desert Motif,'" pp. 37–44. See further his article "Wilderness," *The Interpreter's Dictionary of the Bible, Supplementary Volume*, pp. 946–48.

of life in the promised land. The wilderness is desolate; the land is fertile (Deut. 8:1–10). The wilderness is chaos; the land is rest (*měnûḥāh*, Deut. 12:9).[25]

On the other hand, the wilderness is also the site of divine protection and favor.[26] The pillars of cloud and fire, for example, lead the Israelites day and night. God defeats the Egyptians at the Red Sea and provides water and manna and meat in the barren wilderness. At Mount Sinai in the wilderness he chooses Israel to be his people and establishes a covenant with Israel. In fact, the primary wilderness traditions, according to George Coats' form-critical study, are those which depict a positive relationship between God and Israel. The negative "murmuring" traditions are secondary, originally the product of the Jerusalem cult seeking to stigmatize the North by explaining its defection from the Davidic house with the rebellion in the wilderness.[27]

But it is precisely the retention of the positive tradition of God's aid to Israel in the midst of the negative experience of wilderness which is of interest. The combination of positive and negative characteristics makes the wilderness period an ambiguous place and time, and it is precisely ambiguity that is typical of phenomena of transition, of threshold beings. The wilderness is "betwixt and between," neither here nor there, neither Egypt nor Canaan. It is outside of civilization, remote, harbouring the sacred both divine and demonic. Furthermore, the time spent in the wilderness is "a moment in and out of time." The past is wholly cut off, and the future but faintly envisioned. Slavery is over but freedom is not yet. There God punishes but also protects. The Israelites are in a quarantine chamber, able neither to return to the "house of bondage" nor to proceed directly to the "land of milk of honey." In the schematic forty years, one generation lives and dies apart from time's normal flow. "Your clothing did not wear out upon you, and your foot did not swell, these forty years" (Deut. 8:4). The wilderness time is an eternal present in which the same episodes recur and there is nothing new under the hot desert sun. The wilderness forms the setting for a trek through a time and space apart, ambiguous, liminal.

The second liminal feature of the narrative is the "murmuring" episodes. In each of these episodes the Israelites first "murmur" about lack of food or water or about the untrustworthiness of their leaders. Next Moses responds by crying to God for help. God then imposes a test or

---

[25] See Gerhard von Rad's discussion of this use of *měnûḥāh* in "There Remains Still a Rest for the People of God," *The Problem of the Hexateuch and Other Essays*, trans. E. W. T. Dickens (New York: McGraw-Hill, 1962), pp. 94–102.

[26] In *Rebellion in the Wilderness* (Nashville: Abingdon, 1968), p. 15, George Coats distinguishes sharply between the negative image of wilderness and the positive image of the relationship between God and Israel in the wilderness.

[27] Ibid., pp. 249–54.

ordeal on the community and finally vindicates Moses with a miracle. A symbolic name (e.g., Num. 11:33; 20:13) or cult object (e.g., Exod. 16:32–34; Num. 21:8f.) commemorates the event.[28] Exod. 15:22–26 is a concise example of this pattern:

> When they came to Marah, they could not drink the water of Marah because it was bitter; therefore it was named Marah (bitterness). And the people murmured against Moses, saying, "What shall we drink?" And he cried to the Lord; and the Lord showed him a tree, and he threw it into the water and the water became sweet [vv. 23–25a].

The story goes on to relate that God "tested" (*nissāhû*) them there. Many of the murmuring episodes are more elaborate, yet the basic pattern remains. In several, the frustrations of Moses are emphasized (e.g., Num. 11:11–15), and even God himself is ready to abandon this murmuring people (Num. 14:11f.).

The discipline and patience that these episodes seem designed to inculcate are analogous to the discipline imposed by the elders in the liminal phase of a rite of passage. During this phase the initiates "are being reduced or ground down to a uniform condition to be fashioned anew."[29] Similarly, such trials and frustrations are characteristic of those faced by participants in a social revolution. One thinks, for instance, of Mao's "Long March" and its concomitant deprivations. Of course, the wanderings and trials in the wilderness were "not part of the exodus rhetoric" which seemed to envision a rapid entry into the promised land (Exod. 3:7–8).[30] Unlike the standardized discipline in a rite of passage, the trials in the wilderness appear to be *ad hoc* reactions to Israel's complaints, and the forty year sentence of wandering the culmination of the ordeals which God imposes on the faithless generation (Num. 14:26–35). For the retrospective Deuteronomist, however, the forty years in the wilderness was a necessary stage in the molding of the people: "And you shall remember all the way which the Lord your God has led you these forty years in the wilderness, testing you to know what was in your heart, whether you would keep his commandments or not" (Deut. 8:2).

Although Israel has been freed from bondage in Egypt, the trials in the wilderness serve as the occasion for Israel to learn the lessons of freedom, or, in the words of the folk song, Israel learns that "freedom is another word for nothing left to lose." Through the hardships they endure, the Israelites are purged of their pride, thrown on the mercy of God. They are taught that passivity and humility are the qualities

---

[28]See Jay A. Wilcoxen, "Some Anthropocentric Aspects of Israel's Sacred History," *Journal of Religions* 48 (1968): 341, for a general description of this pattern.

[29]Turner, *The Ritual Process*, p. 95.

[30]Brueggemann, *The Land*, p. 28.

needed to survive in the wilderness.[31] For example, despite human competitiveness, all who collect manna find that in the end they have the same amount, neither too much nor too little. In the face of Miriam's and Aaron's jealous aggressiveness, it is Moses' meekness which is praised. To the spies' evil report of the land, the author opposes the minority report of Caleb and Joshua which proposes to rely on God's aid in the conquest. In each case vulnerability, not pride, is rewarded. Manna, for instance, is pure gift, it cannot be humanly produced or stored, it is peculiar to the wilderness period. It symbolizes the vulnerability of liminality, proving "that man does not live by bread alone, but that man lives by everything that proceeds out of the mouth of the Lord" (Deut. 8:3).

It is the people Israel as a whole which is tested in the wilderness but at the expense of an entire generation which dies there. Turner notes that the ambiguous social status of liminars is often likened to death. In the biblical case the wilderness is preeminently a place of death for Israel, which must die to be reborn. From the Red Sea to the border of Canaan, the Israelites express their certainty of death in the wilderness. In fact, the vociferousness of their "murmuring" about their impending death rises in a steady crescendo. First, on the edge of the wilderness, as Pharaoh's troops bear down on them at the Red Sea, they taunt Moses: "Is it because there are no graves in Egypt that you have taken us away to die in the wilderness? . . . For it would have been better for us to serve the Egyptians than to die in the wilderness" (Exod. 14:11f.). But only two months later, not service in Egypt but death in Egypt looks better to them than the wilderness where Moses has led them "to kill this whole assembly with hunger" (Exod. 16:3). And at Kadesh they lament, "Would that we had died in the land of Egypt! Or would that we had died in this wilderness! Why does the Lord bring us into this land to fall by the sword?" (Num. 14:2f.). Death in Egypt, in the wilderness, in Canaan—the past always seems preferable to the present. Finally, the fear becomes a reality, as the death sentence is passed on the wilderness generation which will wander for forty years "until the last of your dead bodies lies in the wilderness" (Num. 14:33).

Significantly, perhaps, the trek narrative does not relate a single birth. Especially after the emphasis on the amazing fertility of the enslaved Hebrews in Egypt, the silence is striking. The natural process of generation is halted in this time and space apart when Israel is ground down, not built up. Yet as soon as the people cross the Jordan, all those who had been born in the wilderness are circumcised; the natural life cycle resumes (Josh. 5:5–7).

---

[31]Ibid., pp. 30–40, where this point is emphasized. The examples below as well are taken from his discussion.

The trial episodes thus express another facet of the ambiguous quality of liminality, the ambiguity of freedom. En route from one social role to another, from being held by a land to holding a land, the Israelites occupy a precarious status of landlessness. They are free but rootless. They remember longingly the leeks and onions and garlic of Egypt, the wages of slavery, and look ahead to death by the sword in Canaan (Num. 14:3). Egypt, not Canaan, appears to them to be the "land flowing with milk and honey" (Num. 16:13). Only those who learn that freedom means nothing left to lose are ground down sufficiently to experience the other side of freedom, the promised land. Only Joshua and Caleb, the spies with "a different spirit" (Num. 14:24) and the "little ones" (Num. 14:31) will inherit the land.[32] Between the time in which the Hebrews built cities in Egypt in which they would not dwell (Exod. 1:11) and the time in which they dwell in cities in Canaan which they had not built (Deut. 6:10), they are on trial, on the liminal march from slavery to freedom.

The third feature of the wilderness narrative which is characteristic of descriptions of liminal periods is the sacred instruction given on Mount Sinai and the bonds of community it seeks to inculcate. During the liminal phase of initiation rites, the initiates usually receive the law and lore of the society which they are about to enter. Sometimes the information is imparted at hierophanic sites. Sometimes it is accompanied by a "time of marvels," when masked figures appear representing numinous powers and recite myths or reveal *sancta*.[33] The knowledge thus comes as sacred knowledge and binds the initiates together. The climax of a pilgrimage, similarly, is the arrival at the sacred place where the pilgrims experience together a miracle or ritually celebrate a theophany. They emerge newly humbled and united, conscious of a human brotherhood which transcends their class, national, or racial distinctions. The Muslim pilgrimage to Mecca is probably the clearest modern example of a pilgrimage which fosters universal communitas, a blend of "lowliness and sacredness, of homogeneity and comradeship."[34]

The Sinai theophany and the establishment of the covenant are clearly the focus of the entire Pentateuch. To Sinai the fugitive Hebrews march, and from Sinai, as the newly formed people of God, they trek on toward Canaan. Although some critics claim that the Sinai traditions were originally distinct from the exodus, wandering, and conquest traditions and most recognize the varied origins of the legal corpora in the final form of the Pentateuch, the Sinai theophany and covenant

---

[32]Ibid., pp. 38–39.
[33]Turner, *Dramas*, p. 239.
[34]Turner, *The Ritual Process*. p. 96.

have been creatively integrated into the narrative.[35] Two technical considerations show how their positioning in the narrative highlights their function in the sacred history.

First, Frank Moore Cross has shown that the priestly author placed the covenant making at the literary center of the wilderness itinerary.[36] Working from a document which lists forty-two stations in the wilderness, the author created a schema of twelve stations, each introduced by nearly the same formula: "They departed from X and encamped at Y." Before Mount Sinai there are six stations from Egypt to Rephidim, and after Sinai there are six stations to the plains of Moab. Therefore, despite the vast difference in the duration of the journeys between Egypt and Sinai (two months) and between Sinai and Canaan (thirty-eight years), each journey has six camps. The making of the covenant is thus set mytho-geographically at the midpoint of the wilderness.

Second, Jay Wilcoxen points out that the Sinai event divides the murmuring episodes. Before Israel arrives at Mount Sinai, God only reprimands it when it complains, yet after the covenant is made, murmuring results in heavy punishment, usually death. The difference is seen most clearly when one compares similar crises on either side of Sinai (e.g., food in Exodus 16 and Numbers 11; enemies in Exodus 14 and Numbers 14). The covenant is thus seen to mark the definitive beginning of responsibility.[37]

Responsibility is one facet of communitas seen to be engendered by the covenant which binds the people—the Hebrew slaves as well as the mixed multitude—into one nation. Israel responds to God at Sinai with "one voice" (Exod. 24:3). Unlike "natural" communities formed by blood, custom, or conventions, Israel at Sinai is defined by allegiance to God. Apart from the natural and structured societies of Egypt and Canaan, Israel is born. No longer slaves and not yet slave-holders, the Israelites commit themselves to an open society in which ethnic, economic, and social distinctions are minimized. The covenant brotherhood exemplifies Turner's notion of communitas. The Deuteronomist best epitomizes the qualities of "sacredness and lowliness": Israel was the "fewest of peoples," yet chosen to be holy to God (Deut. 7:6f.). The Holiness Code highlights "homogeneity and comradeship": "you shall not take vengeance or bear any grudge against the sons of your own people, but you shall love your neighbor as yourself: I am the Lord" (Lev. 19:18).

[35]Von Rad's essay, "The Form-Critical Problem of the Hexateuch," *The Problem of the Hexateuch and Other Essays*, pp. 1–78, is the classical analysis of the independence of the Sinai traditions. His position is countered by H. Huffmon, "The Exodus, Sinai, and the Credo," *Catholic Biblical Quarterly* 27 (1965): 101–113.

[36]Frank M. Cross, *Canaanite Myth and Hebrew Epic* (Cambridge: Harvard University Press, 1973), p. 308.

[37]Wilcoxen, "Some Anthropocentric Aspects," p. 344.

Although much of the law is devoted to maintaining "structure" in Turner's sense, for instance, by protecting property and establishing priestly privilege, the ethical injunctions strain toward egalitarian communitas. The sabbath legislation, to take the most distinctive example, although presuming a segmented society with servants and resident aliens, insists that sabbath rest applies to all (Exod. 20:8–11). As Brueggemann says, "Sabbath in Israel is the affirmation that people, like land, cannot finally be owned or managed. They are in covenant with us, and therefore lines of dignity and respect and freedom are drawn around them."[38] The Deuteronomic version appends to the sabbath commandment a reminder which punctuates the law like a refrain: "You shall remember that you were servants in the land of Egypt" (Deut. 5:15). Israel's memory of its own servitude stands as a negative example of the inequalities to which a hierarchical society can lead.

In Israelite society no human person or institution is ultimate. The judges are warned: "Justice, and only justice, you shall follow" (Deut. 16:20). The king, too, in the only legislation concerning him, is told to read the law all of his life so "that his heart may not be lifted above his brethren" (Deut. 17:20). The Decalogue, further, prohibits both the anti-divine tendency to pride ("You shall not make for yourself a graven image") and the anti-human tendency to envy ("You shall not covet").[39] The ethics of the Pentateuchal legislation thus witness to the values of communitas which are established in the wilderness.

To summarize, we have seen that the Pentateuchal narrative presents a portrait of Israel in the wilderness in which characteristics of liminality are refracted. The wilderness setting, the trial episodes, and the covenant ethic are analogous to the metaphors and behaviors characteristic of other social and religious phenomena of transition. By retelling, rewriting, and reediting the story of the wilderness trek, the exilic authors gave expression to their own fears and hopes as they re-experienced "liminality" in exile.

However, the claim that the image of Israel in the wilderness is that of a liminal entity needs qualification. We have isolated those features of the narrative which correspond to the conditions of liminality, but other features assert, on the contrary, the value of "structure." Structure is not opposed to communitas in the biblical view but rather completes and guarantees it. In the Pentateuch, law is evaluated positively. It is a gift; it is the barrier against chaos, the antidote to directionlessness. It means "life to you and length of days" (Deut. 30:20). Failure to obey the law will cause the promised land itself to become a wilderness (Deut. 29:23–28). The law makes communitas possible. Spontaneous,

---

[38]Brueggemann, *The Land*, p. 64.

[39]See Eric Voegelin, *Israel and Revelation* (Baton Rouge: Louisiana State University Press, 1956), pp. 425-427.

unregulated behavior in the wilderness leads not to creative encounter but to futile rebellion (Num. 16).

Furthermore, although the law abolishes slavery and envisions equality under God, it legitimates the priestly caste by designating special privileges and responsibilities for Aaron and his family (e.g., Exod. 28–29; Lev. 8–9; Num. 17–18). The revolts against Moses and Aaron may express a "democratic" reaction to authority, but the author regards these actions negatively and thus affirms the privilege of leadership, of social structure.

Therefore, despite the "anti-structure" features of the narrative, it is, at the same time, heavily imbued with the values of structure. By rooting the law in Israel's beginnings in the wilderness, the authors claim that the structured society is the ideal. The seeds of structure are planted in the wilderness but grow only in the land. The Pentateuch's overall evaluation of this time "betwixt and between" is overwhelmingly negative. The trek is a punishment more than a rite of passage; law is salvation more than structural straitjacket. The Pentateuchal vision of the wilderness period is not one of nostalgia for a liminal time to be recaptured but one of hope for its termination.

Although liminal periods are themselves often creative periods, they are not always so viewed. "Liminality may be for many the acme of insecurity, the breakthrough of chaos into cosmos, of disorder into order rather than the milieu of creative interhuman or transhuman achievements. Liminality is both more creative and more destructive than the social norm."[40] Although the wilderness period historically may have been the time when liberation from Egypt gave rise to creative communitas and covenant, it is remembered as the time of disorder which the law redeemed. From their position within "structure," the authors most often view the wilderness as a dangerous place where freedom became license. The authors counter the perceived anarchy of liminality by reading into it the structure of the legal tradition.

Historical Considerations

Is it possible, finally, to move from the literary to the historical level? Do Turner's categories contribute to an appreciation of the social process in Israel? Although they do not further our historical knowledge, they do provide a comparative framework within which the social process in Israel may be understood. We end with three considerations which Turner's study suggests.

First, this reading of the narrative deepens our understanding of the mind-set of the exilic generations. They find themselves "betwixt and between." They are the threshold beings in a time and place apart—in

---

[40]Turner, "Liminal to Liminoid," p. 78.

Babylon—awaiting reentry into the promised land. They are being punished and yet purified through trials and tribulations. They may not survive, but their children, "the little ones," will. As the Holiness Code assures them, "when they are in the land of the enemies, I will not spurn them, neither will I abhor them so as to destroy them utterly and break my covenant with them: for I am the Lord their God" (Lev. 26:45).

Second, this approach may enable us to understand not only the exilic authors but something of the wilderness generation itself. We have claimed, of course, that the wilderness narrative does not directly reflect the historical wilderness period and we have dealt with the paradigmatic qualities of the narrative. Yet Turner's comparative analysis points to the possibility that, despite the long process of transmission, the narrative may well preserve some of the mood or even the conditions of the historical wilderness period. Although the wilderness itinerary may be artificial, the murmuring episodes a literary motif, and the law a later interpolation, it is not at all improbable that the wilderness was the breeding ground for a new socio-religious movement. Between the "structure" of Egypt and the "structure" of Canaan there was a time and space interval of "anti-structure" in which the revolution began. The experiences of freedom and chaos in the wilderness, of hardships and sufferings, and of egalitarian brotherhood, are likely fruits of such an interval. Although the form in which the narrative reflects these features may be late, the experiences themselves are not at all unlikely ones for proto-Israel.

The application of Turner's theory to the wilderness narrative gives support from a history of religions perspective to the similar conclusions reached by Yehezkel Kaufmann from a history of ideas and George Mendenhall from a sociological perspective. Against the regnant thought of his day which subscribed to the gradual evolution of the monotheistic idea, Kaufmann insisted on a "monotheistic revolution" in the wilderness under the leadership of Moses. That the battle against idolatry begins only with Moses warrants the inference that "it was in his time that the great transformation took place."[41] Kaufmann notes that Islam effected a similar kind of revolution. The wholly new religious idea that the deity is ultimate and personal, not subject to a realm of divine fate, and that it is bound to Israel by covenant was an insight that took hold in the wilderness.

More recently, George Mendenhall has offered a new look at the social matrix in which Israel developed. He suggests that "early Israel was the dominion of Yahweh, consisting of all those diverse lineages, clans, individuals, and other social segments that, under the covenant,

---

[41]Yehezkel Kaufman, *The Religion of Israel*, trans. and abr. by Moshe Greenberg, (Chicago: University of Chicago Press, 1960), p. 230.

had accepted the rule of Yahweh and simultaneously had rejected the domination of the various local kings and their tutelary deities—the baalim."[42] These groups had defected from the regnant social structure and joined forces with the nucleus of former Hebrew slaves fired by their experience of God. Again, in this reconstruction the wilderness was the breeding ground for the counter-culture, the communitas destined to attract the disaffected Canaanite marginals. "It was the Mosaic period which constituted revolution; with Solomon the counter revolution triumphed completely, only to collapse under the same weight of political tyranny and arrogance which had so much to do with the troubles of the pre-Mosaic period."[43] Understood through Turner's categories, the wilderness narrative, by depicting the ambiguities of liminality and the energizing force of communitas, presents a plausible picture of the dynamics of such a social and religious revolution.

Third, the biblical historiography subsequent to the wilderness period seems to reflect the dialectic between structure and anti-structure which Turner suggests is characteristic of an enduring social system. Neither structure nor anti-structure is seen as an unmixed blessing. For instance, the stories of the "judges," charismatic warriors who provide *ad hoc* leadership for the loose tribal league, are set in an editorial context which deplores that period in which "there was no king in Israel and every man did what was right in his own eyes" (e.g., Judg. 21:25). Conversely, the positive story of the choice of the first king, Saul, "a head taller than any of the people" (1 Sam. 9:2), is neutralized by Samuel's warning of the dangers of "structure" in Turner's sense, the "ways of the king" who will subject and enslave the people. By Solomon's reign, Israel had transcended the precariousness of wilderness and early settlement life and had reached the full flower of urban civilization. It was a time when "Judah and Israel dwelt in safety, from Dan even to Beersheba, every man under his vine and under his fig tree" (1 Kings 4:24). Yet this golden age of structure was tarnished by the excess of centralized power of which Samuel had warned and by the quashing of the egalitarian, homogeneous society that the covenant had established. On the whole, the prophets reassert the values of communitas over against the pretenses and excesses of the state and the cult, yet they never call for the dissolution of either and for a reversion to the "good old days" in the wilderness.[44]

Thus, this historiography depicts the forces of liminality and communitas oxygenating the heavy atmosphere of structure, as Turner's model might lead us to expect. In the harsh environment of the wilderness,

---

[42]George Mendenhall, *The Tenth Generation* (Baltimore and London: Johns Hopkins University Press, 1973), p. 29.

[43]Ibid., p. 196.

[44]See Talmon, "The Desert Motif," p. 55.

the air was first cleared and the Israelite revolution began. The religious and social values developed during this "moment in and out of time" continued to reassert themselves in later periods. Especially during the exile, the reactualization of liminality drew people to the wilderness story as a paradigm of their own experience. Yet the interpretation of law and liminality in the trek narrative shows that the authors perceived the period to be a crucible in which the right mixure of structure and anti-structure was forged. The narrative thus became a repository for traditions expressing the amibiguities of liminality, the possibilities of communitas, and the limiting values of structure. In the elaboration of this story the religious imagination continued to identify the precarious-ness and the promise of being Israel.

Chapter Three

MOUNTAINS IN THE BIBLICAL COSMOS

Like most archaic peoples, ancient Israel lived close to its land. Biblical writers marvel at the contours and contrasts of the land of Israel, at its hills and valleys, its forests and deserts, its rivers and streams. From the "travelogue" of the patriarchs, to the "atlas" of the conquest, to the "pastorale" of the prophets, the Bible attends to the topography, extent, and condition of the land. Since our natural environment affects the way we look at the world, surely, for geographically sensitive Israel, the shape of its land helped to shape its perceptions. The student of religions, therefore, must take account of geographic factors in its effort to understand the dynamics of the biblical imagination.[1]

Outstanding among the topographical features of the land of Israel are its mountains and hills, and these, appropriately, receive prominent attention in biblical literature. Not only do mountains figure significantly in the historical narratives, but they are used frequently in poetic imagery. Mountains, moreover, capture the religious imagination as places where the divine touches the human sphere. Among the several mountains likely regarded as sacred in ancient Israel, Mount Sinai and Mount Zion emerge as the two pivots of biblical sacred history. The Bible thus reflects Israel's consciousness of mountains in several ways: mountains are physical reality, literary motif, and sacred space.

In this essay we analyze the mountain motif and show it to be an important ingredient of the poetic depiction of Mount Zion. Symbols, Clifford Geertz says, are "collectively created patterns of meaning the individual uses to give form to experience and point to action."[2] Contributing to the "pattern of meaning" which is Mount Zion is the biblical perception of mountains in general. And underlying this perception is the geophysical reality of Israel. Thus the mountain motif arises, at least in part, from mountain reality and finds fullest expression in the

---

[1] For a good discussion of the relation of geography to world-view and a suggestive case study, see Klimkeit, "Spatial Orientation in Mythical Thinking as Exemplified in Ancient Egypt," pp. 266–81.

[2] Clifford Geertz, *Islam Observed* (Chicago and London: University of Chicago Press, 1968), p. 95.

symbolically conceived Mount Zion. Accordingly, we first sketch the role of the mountain in Israelite history and, second, discuss the major images which are components of the mountain motif. Finally, we demonstrate that these images are reconfigured in the Zion symbol.

Mountain Reality

First, a word or two about the Hebrew terms for "mountain" will indicate the extent of biblical references to mountain phenomena.[3] The most common word for mountain, *har*, appears five hundred and twenty times in the Bible (in every book except Ruth, Ecclesiastes, Esther, and Ezra) and has two basic meanings. First, it refers to a hilly or mountainous region (e.g., *har yĕhûdāh*, "the hill country of Judah"). In fact, in two instances poets apparently use the word *har* to denote the land of Israel as a whole (Exod. 15:17; Ps. 78:54). Second, it signifies a specific mountain, named or unnamed. Twenty-three individual mountains have proper names, ranging in height from the lofty Mount Lebanon (3000 meters) and Mount Hermon (2760 meters) to the tiny Mount Zion (743 meters), only 50 meters above the adjacent Kidron valley.

The second most frequent term, *gib'āh* (sixty times), is usually translated as "hill." Chiefly a poetic designation, it appears thirty-nine times in the Latter Prophets, but only twelve times in the historical books. The word *gib'āh* appears to have the same meaning as *har* with two exceptions: it may be lower in height; and it always denotes a single hill, never a range of hills. In biblical poetry, *har* and *gib'āh* in their plural forms constitute a hendiadys, a "fixed-pair."[4] The members of the pair are used together, "mountains and hills" (e.g., Ezek. 6:3), or, in thirty-one instances, in "break-up pattern" in parallel cola of a couplet (e.g., Jer. 4:24; Hab. 3:6). In these cases, *hārîm* and *gĕbā'ôt* are synonymous.

In addition, several other words that appear in poetic synonymous parallelism with *har* or *gib'āh* most likely denote "mountain" on these occasions.[5] The Semitic cognates of *ṣûr*, "rock," (Ugaritic *ġr*; Aramaic *tùr*), *śādeh*, "field," (Akkadian *šadu*), and *gĕbûl*, "border," (Arabic

---

[3] The brief summary in this paragraph is adapted from A. Schwarzenbach, *Die Geographische Terminologie im Hebraischen des Alten Testaments* (Leiden: Brill, 1954), pp. 6–7. See also S. Talmon, "*har*; *gibh'āh*," *Theological Dictionary of the Old Testament*, Vol. III, ed. G. Johannes Botterweck and Helmer Ringgren, trans. David E. Green (Grand Rapids, Mich.: Eerdmans, 1978), pp. 431–47.

[4] For studies of hendiadys and its break-up pattern see R. G. Boling, "'Synonymous' Parallelism in the Psalms." *Journal of Semitic Studies* 5 (1960): 221–25; S. Gevirtz, *Patterns in the Early Poetry of Israel* (Chicago: University of Chicago Press, 1963); E. J. Melamed, "Break-up of Stereotype Phrases as an Artistic Device in Biblical Poetry," *Scripta Hierosolymitana* 8 (Jerusalem: Magnes, 1964): 115–44.

[5] See S. Talmon, "*har*; *gibh'āh*," pp. 431–32.

ğabal) are the standard words for mountains in their respective languages.[6] The parallel *ṣûr/har* (e.g., Job 14:8; Num. 23:9) is especially interesting in light of the divine epithet *ṣûr yiśrā'ēl*, which may be rendered "mountain of Israel."[7] Finally, the words *bāmāh*, "high place," and *mārôm*, "height," are sacred as well as geographical designations. *Bāmāh* generally denotes the hilltop altars of pagan fertility cults (e.g., 2 Kings 23:15), while *mārôm* indicates Yahweh's heavenly or earthly dwelling place.[8] Of the many terms which refer to specific features of mountains, several are analogues to features of human or animal anatomy. A mountain's summit is its "head" (*r'oš*); a peak is a "tooth" (*šēn*); a slope is a "shoulder" (*ketep*, *šĕkem*).[9] These designations may be mythological remnants or merely poetic personification. In any case, the wealth of Hebrew terminology for "mountain" indicates the biblical sensitivity to the phenomenon. A brief look at the role of mountains in Israelite history will help to explain this sensitivity.

From its earliest days the Israelite settlement in Canaan was identified with the central mountain range west of the Jordan and with the trans-Jordanian highlands east of the river. Egyptian documents list many Canaanite fortified city-states on the seacoast and in the Jordan and Jezreel valleys, but very few in the hill country which the Israelite tribes occupied. Indeed, it is likely that Israelite tribes rapidly penetrated and consolidated in Canaan because the hill country which they settled had been sparsely occupied.[10] In fact, it seems to have been largely forested, for Joshua orders the tribe of Joseph to clear the forested hills to make room for itself (Josh. 17:17–18). Moreover, Canaanite cities in the plains remained after I sraelite settlement in the hills. Judah, for example, "took possession of the hill country, but could not drive out the inhabitants of the plains because they had chariots of iron" (Judg. 1:19).[11]

---

[6] Passages where these words appear in parallel with *har* are Job 14:18; Num. 23:9 (*ṣûr*); Deut. 32:13; Judg. 5:4 (*śādeh*); Ps. 78:54 (*gĕbûl*).

[7] See the discussion of David Sperling, "Mount, mountain," *The Interpreter's Dictionary of the Bible, Supplementary Volume*, pp. 608–609.

[8] A *bāmāh*, however, need not be located on a hill. The *bāmāh* of Topeth stood in the valley of Ben Hinnom in Jerusalem (Jer. 7:31; 32:35). See Roland de Vaux, *Ancient Israel*, (New York and Toronto: McGraw Hill, 1965), 2:284.

[9] These terms occur in Gen. 8:5 (*r'oš*); 1 Sam. 14:4 (*šēn*); Num. 34:11 (*ketep*); Gen. 48:22 (*šĕkem*). See Talmon, "*har; gibh'āh*," p. 432.

[10] Egyptian execration texts (20–19th centuries B. C. E.), Amarna letters (14th century B.C.E.), and other inscriptions and papyrii suggest that the Canaanite cities were never united but remained under Egyptian suzerainty. Jerusalem and Shechem were apparently the only sizable Canaanite settlements in the hill country, and the kings of those cities dominated wide areas of sparsely inhabited land. See Y. Aharoni, *The Land of the Bible: A Historical Geography*, trans. A. F. Rainey (London: Burns and Oates, 1967), pp. 131–64, esp. pp. 157–64.

[11] The Danites may later have migrated northward in part because they were unable to control the plains. "The Amorites pressed the Danites back into the hill country for they did not allow them to come down in the plain" (Judg. 1:34).

The Philistine threat, which unified the tribes and spurred the creation of the monarchy, was perceived to be the encroachment of a plains people into Israel's mountain territory. The Philistines "went up against Israel" (1 Sam. 7:7), while Saul advises Israel: "Let us go down after the Philistines by night" (1 Sam. 14:36). Although until his death Saul apparently kept the Philistines out of the hill country, it remained for David to defeat them decisively (2 Sam. 8:1). Under David's leadership, Israel first moved out of the hill country, for David conquered the Canaanite cities on the plains and made vassals of the states east of the Jordan. The hill country thus served as the base from which Israel descended to conquer the plains and unite the land for the first time into a single political unit.[12]

Even after the Israelite empire was established, however, the old hill country identification persisted. The names of Solomon's twelve administrative districts, for instance, are divided evenly between names of Canaanite cities in the plains and names of Israelite tribes in the hills (1 Kings 4:7–19).[13] Also, Omri's purchase of the hill of Shemer for his new capital (1 Kings 16:24) indicates the continuing strategic importance of hills. Israel's neighbors, furthermore, considered Israel a hill people, for as late as Ahab's reign the servants of the king of Syria advise him: "Their gods are gods of the hills, and so they were stronger than we; but let us fight against them in the plain, and surely we shall be stronger than they" (1 Kings 20:23).

Indeed, the agriculture of early Israel reveals that its land base was in the hill country. Grain growing in the valleys, and vineyards and olive trees on the hillsides stand behind the popular summary of Israel's major products: "the grain, the wine, and the oil" (e.g., Deut. 28:51; Jer. 31:12; 2 Chron. 31:5).[14] Complementing hillside agriculture are the frequently mentioned professions of herding and shepherding (e.g., Deut. 7:13; 18:4; Jer. 31:12). Another formula, "land of milk and honey" (e.g., Exod. 3:8; Deut. 6:3), suggests the combination of agriculture and livestock, for milk represents dairy products from flocks and herds, while honey derives from date trees on the hillsides.[15] In short, Israel's political and economic life was centered in the hill country.

[12] See Aharoni, *The Land of the Bible*, p. 220.

[13] The first name in the list is Mount Ephraim, followed by six Canaanite cities and five tribes. If Mount Ephraim is taken to mean the whole Ephraim-Manasseh hill country, it can be added to the names of the tribes to produce a six-six division. See Aharoni, *The Land of the Bible*, pp. 277–80, for a full analysis of the list.

[14] A more complete list of products is found in Deut. 8:7–8 where the "seven species" of agriculture are mentioned.

[15] See Aharoni, *The Land of the Bible*, p. 14.

The Mountain Motif

Having established the importance of mountains in Israelite language and life, we turn to the mountain motif in biblical literature. The sources of literary imagery are not easy to trace. Much imagery is simply traditional, formulaic. Thus, as J.J.M. Roberts notes, in personal names dating to the third millenium in the ancient Near East, words for mountain are used as metaphors for a place of refuge.[16] Still, even if imagery does not arise directly from experience, it is used because it crystallizes experience. For instance, however formulaic or hackneyed it may sound today to say "the Lord is my shepherd," the image has resonated with countless generations because it has expressed their experience of divine nurture, guidance, and protection. The Israelites surely were struck by the security which their mountains afforded, by the majesty of the surrounding ranges, and by the fertility of their hilly homeland. Such perceptions may well be the basis of three major foci of mountain imagery: mountains are renowned for their security, their height, and their fertility.

Security

It is easy to see, first of all, why mountains would function as images of security. They are often difficult to penetrate and to climb, and their rocks and caves provide hiding places for fugitives. Indeed, the Israelites hide from the Midianites in "the dens which are in the mountains" (Judg. 6:2). Similarly, when Sodom and Gomorrah are destroyed, Lot and his daughters flee to the hills (Gen. 19:17). People attempt to escape even God's wrath by taking refuge in the mountains, yet "though they hide themselves on the top of Carmel, / from there I will search out and take them" (Amos 9:3).[17] Here the mountaintop becomes a hyperbole for the most distant hiding place.

The mountains are also associated with the protection which Yahweh provides. The psalmist reflects, "I will lift my eyes to the hills, from where my help comes" (Ps. 121:1). Interpreters divide on the meaning of this oft-quoted verse, but whether the "mountains" referred to are earthly or celestial, they here promise divine help.[18] In fact, the word ṣûr, "rock," sometimes a synonym for mountain, is an epithet for Yahweh himself in his function as protector. Yahweh is the "ṣûr of my

---

[16] Personal communication.

[17] Similarly, in the Baal epic, when Baal gives forth his voice against his enemies, "Baal's enemies take to the woods / Hadd's foes to the sides of the mountain" (II AB vii 34f.). See James Pritchard, *Ancient Near Eastern Texts Relating to the Old Testament*, 3d ed. with Supplement (Princeton: Princeton University Press, 1969), p. 135.

[18] See Mitchell Dahood, *Psalms III: 101–150*, The Anchor Bible, (Garden City: Doubleday, 1970), p. 200.

salvation" (2 Sam. 22:47; cf. 22:32; 23:3), "my *ṣûr*, my fortress, my deliverer" (Ps. 18:3). Another psalm depicts a person in dire straits begging for God to "lead me to the *ṣûr* that is higher than I" (Ps. 61:3). Dahood renders this clause as "lead me to the Lofty Mountain," finding here an epithet for Yahweh's celestial abode.[19] If he is right, the mountain is here, too, connected with divine protection.

Biblical cosmology provides another context in which imagery of security appears. The mountains are noted as a constituent element of creation, though distinguished for their power and permanence. Although the Genesis creation account makes no mention of the mountains, they are prominent in the older poetic tradition preserved in several psalms and in Job. In the beginning God "established the mountains, being girded with might" (Ps. 65:7). Unlike the chaotic, roaring sea (v. 8), the mountains are steady and silent. They stand firm as a testimony to the orderliness of creation. The chaos became cosmos, in another psalm (104:5-8), when the primeval waters fled in fear of God, exposing an earth of mountains and valleys. Here, as well, the mountains support life. The rivers flow between them (v. 10), and the wild goats roam contentedly upon them (v. 18), for there the fructifying rain falls (v. 13).

Elsewhere, the mountains are singled out for their antiquity; they are a standard against which permanence is measured. For instance, Eliphaz taunts Job: "Are you the first man that was born, or were you made before the hills?" (Job 15:7). "Wisdom," indeed, boasts: "Before the *hārîm* had been shaped, / before the *gĕbā'ôt*, I was brought forth" (Prov. 8:25). Similarly, a psalmist conceives of the eternity of God by proclaiming that God existed even before the mountains: "Before the mountains were brought forth / or ever thou hadst formed the earth and the world, / from everlasting to everlasting thou art God" (Ps. 90:3). The mountains are thus conceived to be the oldest, most secure, element of the cosmos. In fact, mountains can even represent the cosmos as a whole. In Micah's "covenant lawsuit" God calls upon the mountains and hills to witness his case against Israel: "Arise, plead your case before the mountains, / and let the hills hear your voice" (Mic. 6:1).[20] Like "heaven and earth," the more usual ear to God's testimony (e.g., Deut. 32:1), "mountains and hills" is a shorthand expression for the cosmos. Whereas in Hittite covenant treaties, for instance, the gods serve as witnesses, here where the covenant signatories are God and Israel, the cosmos fills the role of permanent witness.

---

[19] Mitchell Dahood, *Psalms II: 51–100*, The Anchor Bible (Garden City: Doubleday, 1968), p. 85.

[20] See G. E. Wright, "The Lawsuit of God: A Form-Critical Study of Deuteronomy 32," *Israel's Prophetic Heritage: Essays in Honor of James Muilenberg*, ed. B. W. Anderson (New York: Harper, 1962), pp. 26–67.

Finally, the permanence of the mountains is underscored, negatively, in depictions of Yahweh's wrath. Here, nothing stands before Yahweh, the "divine warrior," when he marches against his enemies, be they the powers of Sheol, the enemies of Israel, or Israel itself. *Even the mountains*, a touchstone of security, do not remain steady. "The mountains melt like wax before the Lord" (Ps. 97:5). Yahweh dries up the rivers and seas, dessicates Bashan, Carmel, and Lebanon, and "the mountains quake before him" (Nah. 1:4f.). The earth shakes and "the eternal mountains were scattered, / the everlasting hills sank low" (Hab. 3:6). All of the cosmos convulses and the mountains along with it. Although biblical authors see in the mountains a main witness to the order and permanence of the created world, mountains, like the rest of nature, remain dependent upon the creator for their continued existence.

Height

Mountains are impressive, most of all, because of their physical dimensions. They have summoned countless explorers, inspired poets, attracted saints. Biblical authors also express the awe of the Israelites before mountain heights. The psalmist who lifts his eyes to the hills (Ps. 121:1) does so because their height points to divinity. Another, praising God's creation, declares: "in his hand are the depths of the earth; / the heights of the mountains are his also" (Ps. 95:4). In biblical cosmology the mountains are noted not only for their height but also for their depth, for they reach down to the foundations of the earth.[21] Jonah finds himself at the mountain bottoms deep in the sea (Jon. 2:7), and the "foundations of the hills" (Ps. 18:8) tremble when God is angry.

Mountain heights are closely associated with authority. The signal illustration, of course, is the law-giving on Mount Sinai where Yahweh appears dramatically and uniquely (see chapter four). The authority of mountains also undergirds the ceremony of divine blessing and curse set between mounts Gerizim and Ebal (Deut. 11:26–32; 27:11–13; cf. Josh. 8:30–35).[22] Here, in a performance apparently related to a covenant renewal, half of the Levites stand upon Gerizim to recite blessings for those who adhere to the covenant and half stand upon Ebal to recite

---

[21] See Talmon's discussion of the "world axis" in "*har; gibh'āh*," p. 439–40.

[22] The logistics and meaning of the ceremony are far from clear. The several references to it in Deuteronomy and Joshua do not agree. It does appear, however, that the blessing and curse are not set upon but rather delivered from the mountains. The expression *nātattā . . . 'al* (Deut. 11:29) which the Revised Standard Version translates "set . . . on [the mountain]" is better rendered "given, delivered on" (cf. Jer. 4:16; 22:20 "utter"; Neh. 5:7; Ps. 148:6 "make"). A study of the ceremony is included in Eduard Nielsen, *Shechem: A Traditio-Historical Investigation* (Copenhagen: G. E. C. Gad, 1955), pp. 68–69.

curses for disobedience. The people, gathered in the valley between the mountains, answer "Amen," accepting the choice set before them.

In addition to these examples, where specific mountains evoke divine power, the literary convention of the mountain address illustrates the more general association of authority with peaks. From any high place, of course, one has a commanding view of one's audience; one can see and be seen. Biblical orators often speak from the heights of an acropolis or a city wall; from there their words carry authority.[23] Similarly, the mountaintop speech became a typical way of conveying divine anger or pleasure. For instance, from the top of Mount Gerizim, Jotham curses the men of Shechem for their support of Abimelekh who murdered his brothers and usurped the kingship (Judg. 9:7). Similarly, from Mount Zemaraim, Abijah denies Jeroboam's legitimacy and promises Israel's defeat (2 Chron. 13:4–12). In both cases, the curse from the mountain takes effect because it carries divine sanction. Of course, from a mountain peak such as Gerizim a speaker could not be heard in the valley below; therefore, it is clear that the mountain setting is a literary device.

Not only curse but also blessing is proclaimed from the mountaintop. In the Balaam stories, the Moabite king summons the pagan prophet Balaam to curse Israel from the peak of Bamot-Baal ("high places of Baal"), but Balaam utters a blessing instead, for he can only "speak what the Lord puts in my mouth" (Num. 23:12). Twice more, atop Pisgah and Peor, Balak's plan is foiled when Balaam blesses Israel. Throughout, the author stresses Balak's insistence that Balaam see the enemy he is to curse. Accordingly, the mountaintops provide progressively wider views of Israel (22:41; 23:13; 24:2), yet these views call forth blessing rather than curse. Finally, on the last mountain, Balaam's eyes are "uncovered" (24:4,16) and he sees into time as well, for he proclaims the glorious future of Israel. The mountain height here thus calls forth spiritual sight.

Another literary convention associates the height of the mountains with human pride and arrogance. Yahweh is preeminently associated with height: he dwells "in a high (*mārôm*) and holy place" (Isa. 57:15), on a throne "high and lifted up" (Isa. 6:1); he alone is the "high tower" (Ps. 62:3). He controls the heights; therefore, the idolatrous worship on the "high places" (*bāmôt*) and "on every high hill and under every green tree" are an especial affront.[24] On the "day of Yahweh" he will have revenge

---

[23] See M. Weinfeld, *Deuteronomy and the Deuteronomic School* (Oxford: Oxford University Press, 1972), pp. 176–77. Examples are found in Prov. 1:21; 9:3.

[24] See W. L. Holladay, "On Every High Hill and Under Every Green Tree," *Vetus Testamentum* 11 (1961): 170–76 for a discussion of the phrase.

against all that is proud and lofty . . .
against all the cedars of Lebanon
   lofty and lifted up . . .
against all the high mountains,
   and against all the lofty hills [Isa. 2:12–14].

This litany of high and exalted things culminates in the haughtiness of man (v. 17). Applied to humans, height is negative; high mountains remind the poet of human self-exaltation.

Because high mountains are associated with human pride, ascent of the mountain is a figure for human challenge to divine authority.[25] Sennacherib of Assyria, for instance, is said to have "mocked the Lord" when he claimed, "With my many chariots I have gone up to the heights of the mountains ($měrôm hārîm$), / to the extremities of ($yarkětê$) Lebanon" (Isa. 37:24). Sennacherib's boasting, Isaiah taunts, will come to naught. Obadiah, similarly, portrays the Edomites resting securely in their mountainous land:

The pride of your heart has deceived you,
   you who live in the clefts of the rock,
   whose dwelling is high,
   who say in your heart,
"Who will bring me down to the ground?" [Obad. 3].

Yet Yahweh declares, "I will bring you down" (v. 4). Here the actual terrain of Edom has prompted the nation, in Obadiah's view, to think of itself as "high," exalted. Although Edom may be ascendant after Babylon's sacking of Jerusalem, ultimately, "Saviours shall go up to Mount Zion to rule Mount Esau" (v. 21). Obadiah thus depicts the struggle between the nations as the conflicts between two mountains.

In addition, two prophetic oracles show foreign kings committing *hybris* by ascending not simply the mountains in general but the "mountain of God." Isaiah accuses the king of Babylon of saying,"I will ascend to heaven; / above the stars of God; / I will set my throne on high; / I will sit on the mount of assembly on the extremities ($běyarkětê$) of Zaphon" (14:13). Here, confusingly, the Canaanite idea of the mount of assembly of the god El appears to be joined with Zaphon, the mountain of Baal. (Israelites, it seems, interpreted Canaanite mythology quite freely!)[26] In its biblical context, however, it is clear that the king aspires to be like God by sitting on his mountain. Yet he will be brought down to the "extremities of ($yarkětê$) the pit," Sheol (v. 15). In another oracle, Ezekiel tells of the king of Tyre, who was set on the "holy mountain of God" located in "Eden, the garden of God"

[25] S. Talmon suggested to me the metaphor and several of the examples below. See now his "$har; gibh'āh$," pp. 441–42.

[26] See the comments of J. J. M. Roberts, "The Davidic Origin of the Zion Tradition," *Journal of Biblical Literature* 92 (1973): 341–42.

(Ezek. 28:13f.) and adorned with precious stones. This favored position led to his self-exaltation, and he was "cast as a profane thing from the mountain of God" (28:16). Although the variety of mythological motifs conjoined in these oracles complicates their meaning, in both cases foreign kings overstep the bounds of kingship when they try to use the mountain of God as a catapult to divine prerogative. No faithful Israelite is ever so portrayed.

A variation on this same theme, Talmon suggests, is the tower of Babel story. The people of the earth seek to protect themselves from God, to make themselves a "name" (Gen. 11:4), and so they build a city and a tower "with its top in the heavens." Here an artifical mountain is a means to power and control. God, however, responds to this human attempt to ascend by descending and scattering the people; and, as a result, the project is left unfinished. The abandoned tower testifies to the futility of pre-Israelite efforts to shut God out. Moreover, the tower, "Babel," probably satirizes the Babylonian ziggurats, the temple towers upon which the priests approached the gods.[27] Here the ziggurat is identical with "confusion," a model of foreign folly.

To summarize, in the biblical cosmos, height imagery not only witnesses to the majesty of Yahweh's creation but points to Yahweh himself. The mountains, indeed, extend from the heavens, Yahweh's abode, to the foundations of the earth. Because of the sense of authority which they evoke, mountains are used as settings from which Yahweh's spokesmen deliver his blessings and curses. Yet mountain height is also a metaphor for arrogant human pride; divine challengers cannot successfully climb the mountain of God.

Fertility

Fertility is the third locus of mountain imagery. Biblical authors rejoiced in the fertility of their land and saw in its forested hills and green valleys clear evidence of divine favor. Unlike the land of Egypt, the promised land "is a land of hills and valleys which drinks water by the rain from heaven, a land which the Lord your God cares for" (Deut. 11:11f.). Similarly, the psalmist declares, "From thy lofty abode thou waterest the mountains; / the earth is satisfied with the fruit of thy work" (Ps. 104:13). When biblical authors reflect upon the fertility of the land, they thus think of its hilly character. In fact, the frequent use

---

[27] The link between the mountain motif, the tower, and the Babylonian ziggurat is suggested in at least two other biblical allusions. First, in Jer. 51:25 Babylon is dubbed "destroying mountain," perhaps a reference to the ziggurat. Second, E. J. Hamlin argues that the mountains and hills to be "threshed" and destroyed in Isa. 41:14–16 are Mesopotamian ziggurats, particularly the one in the city of Babylon itself. "The Meaning of Mountains and Hills in Isa. 41:14–16," *Journal of Near Eastern Studies* 13 (1954): 185–90.

of the word pair *'ereṣ/hārîm*, "earth/mountains," suggests that in biblical literary language the hills and the land are practically synonymous (cf. Isa. 14:25; Nah. 1:5; Pss. 18:8; 46:3; 72:16).

The covenant between Yahweh and Israel implicates the land and, thus, the mountains as well. Israel's hold on the land of Canaan and the fertility of the land are contingent upon Israel's faithfulness to its covenant obligations (Lev. 26:3–5; Deut. 11:13–15). Furthermore, according to the royal ideology, when the righteous king executes justice in the land, Israel can expect the land to be so fertile that flax, which normally grows in the plains will wave "on the tops of the mountains" (Ps. 72:16).[28] Conversely, when Israel breaks the covenant, "the land shall not yield its increase" (Lev. 26:20). Isaiah threatens that "all the hills which used to be hoed with a hoe ... will become a place where cattle are let loose and where sheep tread" (Isa. 7:24f.) because of the briers and thorns that will grow there. After the exile, Haggai declares "a drought upon the land and upon the mountains" (Hag. 1:11) for the people's failure to rebuild the temple. The fertility of the land and its hills is God's instrument for rewarding or punishing Israel.

The mountains, moreover, actually share in Israel's punishment and reward. In a literary apostrophe, Ezekiel addresses the mountains of Israel and proclaims that they will suffer for their sins:

> Son of man, set your face toward the mountains of Israel, and prophesy against them, and say: Mountains of Israel, hear the word of the Lord! Thus says the Lord God to the mountains and the hills, to the ravines and the valleys: Behold I, even I, will bring a sword upon you, and I will destroy your high places [6:2f].

The mountains themselves are guilty because of the *bāmôt*, "high places," upon them, so the altars will be broken and dead bodies strewn around them (vv. 4f.). Mountains and people have conspired against Yahweh and his revenge must be upon both. Similarly, Ezekiel expands an oracle against Edom (25:12–14) into an apostrophe against Mount Seir, another epithet (like Mount Esau in Obadiah) for the land of Edom (Ezek. 35). Because the Edomites gloated over Judah's defeat by Babylon and put the survivors to the sword, Mount Seir will be made "a desolation and a waste" (v. 3). Its dead will lie on the mountains and hills and valleys and ravines (v. 8). Ezekiel even depicts the wicked aims of the Edomites as Mount Seir "reviling" the mountains of Israel (v. 12).

On the other hand, the mountains share also in triumph. Renewed fertility of the land of Israel will accompany the restoration of the people

---

[28] A rabbinic saying catches this hyperbole: "Our rabbis taught: 'There will be a rich cornfield upon the top of the mountains.' From this it was inferred that there will be a time when wheat will rise as high as a palm tree and will grow on top of the mountains" (*b.Ketubot* 111b). *The Talmud*, trans. I. Slotski (London: Soncino, 1936), 18:720–21.

of Israel to it. Thus, juxtaposed to Ezekiel's curse on Mount Seir is his blessing upon the mountains of Israel (Ezek. 36): "But you, O mountains of Israel, shall shoot forth your branches, and yield your fruit to my people Israel; for they will soon come home. For I am for you, and I will turn to you, and you shall be tilled and sown. . . ." (vv. 8f). Restoration is envisioned as new creation: both man (*'ādām*) and beast are to "multiply and be fruitful" just as in the Genesis creation story. The mountains once cursed (Ezek. 6) are now blessed with new productivity.

Other prophets, as well, promise new fertility for the mountains as a sign of restoration. Jeremiah sees vineyards again planted upon the mountains of Samaria (Jer. 31:4). According to Amos, "the mountains shall drip sweet wine, / and all the hills will flow with it" (Amos 9:13). The grapes need not even ferment! Similarly, Joel's hyperbole has the hills flowing with milk (4:18). The mountains join with the rest of the cosmos in singing praises to Yahweh for the new creation, Israel reborn (Isa. 49:11). The richness and wide distribution of the imagery indicates the extent to which poets felt the mountains of Israel were linked intimately to the fate of the people.

The association of the mountains with fertility leads to two further literary uses of mountains: as a negative metaphor for pagan fertility cults and as a positive metaphor for human fertility. Sexual rites, first of all, were an important part of the religion of Canaan because ritual intercourse in the Canaanite view helped to maintain the fertility of the earth. Sacred prostitution seems to have been practiced in the Israelite cult as well, even in the Jerusalem house of Yahweh.[29] The prophets, especially Hosea and Jeremiah, strongly condemn such practices as "harlotry" (e.g., Hos. 9:1f.; Jer. 5:7). Naturally, fertile hilltops were frequent settings for this worship.

> They sacrifice on the tops of the mountains,
>   and make offerings upon the hills,
> under oak, poplar, and terebinth,
>   because their shade is good.
> Therefore your daughters play the harlot
>   and your brides commit adultery . . .
> the men themselves go aside with harlots,
>   and sacrifice with cult prostitutes [Hos. 4:13f.].

The "high places" where such worship occurred were frequently located on uninhabited hilltops. In fact, Jeremiah alludes to the fertility cult with the formula "on every high hill and under every green tree" (e.g., 2:20). The prophets give the impression that sexual rites dominated Israelite religion. Ironically, however, the hilltop "harlotry" pollutes

---

[29] See Samuel Terrien, "The Omphalos Myth and Hebrew Religion," *Vetus Testamentum* 20 (1970): 326–27.

rather than fertilizes the land (Jer. 3.2). The "hills," therefore, come to be associated with illicit fertility rites.

In contrast to this negative connotation is the positive use of mountains as metaphors for female fertility in the Song of Songs. Here mountains, named and unnamed, evoke a variety of pictures. The poet, for instance, compares the woman's hair to a flock of goats moving down Gilead (4:1=6:5) and her head to Carmel (7:5). Carmel, overlooking the sea and renowned for its fertile pasturage, suggests both the prominence of the head and its luxuriant growth of flowing hair. Lebanon, mentioned seven times, is renowned for its fragrant forest and flowing streams; these features point metaphorically to the woman's perfumed fragrance and her liquid resources.

The hendiadys "mountains and hills" appears here in a wholly new context. First, the man is pictured as a gazelle "leaping upon the mountains, / bounding over the hills" in pursuit of his beloved (2:8f.). It is doubtful that the poet has in mind here only the breathless run of the lover through the mountains. Mountains and hills may also stand for parts of the female body, as the next reference to mountains suggests:

> Until the day breathes,
>> and the shadows flee,
> turn, my beloved, be like a gazelle,
>> or a young stag upon "cleft" mountains [hārê bāter] [2:17].

Although the meaning of the last phrase is disputed, the "mountains" here refer more clearly to the woman than in 2:8. The "cleft" mountains, says Marvin Pope, may refer to "the breast, *mons Veneris* or other bifurcated charms of the bride."[30] The third reference to mountains clinches the identification of mountains with female fertility, for after he has described his beloved's charms, the lover proclaims, "I will hie me to the mountain of myrhh / and the hill of frankincense" (4:6). Here the curvacious and fragrant woman herself is likened to a mountain, or, perhaps, her breasts are the mountains of spices. The final verse in the book combines the images of 2:17 and 4:6, for the lover is invited to "be like a gazelle" (2:17) "upon the mountains of spices," the myrrh and frankincense of 4:6. In this poetic anthology, then, the mountains are a fertile source of erotic imagery.

In sum, the mountains are fertile because they are the foremost feature of the fertile promised land. Their fertility, however, depends upon Israel's obedience or the king's righteousness. In fact, poets such as Ezekiel picture the mountains reflecting Israel's triumph and tragedy

---

[30] Marvin Pope, *Song of Songs*, The Anchor Bible (Garden City: Doubleday, 1977), p. 410.

in their fertility or aridness. Finally, mountain fertility stands behind metaphors for illicit sexual rites and for human fertility.

Mount Zion

We have seen the variety of roles which the mountains play in the biblical imagination. They serve as images of security, permanence, and antiquity, yet they tremble at God's wrath. They link Yahweh's abode with the human realm on earth; thus, they are common settings for authoritative decrees. Their natural fertility is praised, while the fertility rites associated with them are condemned. They even become metaphors for female pulchritude.

These images of security, height, and fertility, associated with the mountains in general, conjoin in the biblical description of Mount Zion. In their creation of this sacred symbol, biblical poets drew upon the traditional mountain motif. Because of its new status as Yahweh's chosen abode, Mount Zion became the locus of security, height, and fertility in the eyes of the poets. In the symbol "Mount Zion," then, the mountain motif finds new application and configuration.

Of course, the mountain motif is only one element of the "pattern of meaning" which the symbol represents. As we shall see in chapter four, Mount Sinai imagery, too, was transferred to Mount Zion. Biblical poets also "borrowed" from the Canaanite sacred mountan traditions associated with the gods Baal and El.[31] Further, they may have inherited Zion traditions from their Jebusite predecessors in Jerusalem.[32] Yet, whatever was "borrowed" functioned independently of its origin. The sacred montain symbol, in order to work, had to "give form to experience." Mount Zion thus attracted the images of security, height, and fertility, which were elements of the biblical conceptualization of the mountains in general. Let us survey the manner in which Mount Zion projects these images.

First, as the home of the eternal God, Mount Zion is itself eternal. The psalms, accordingly, reflect not the historical past when David captured the city Jerusalem but rather the eternal present in which Yahweh reigns from Mount Zion. "His abode is in Salem, / his den is in Zion" (Ps. 76:2f.). In fact, the eternality of Zion suggests Yahweh's protection of the faithful, for "those who trust in the Lord are like Mount Zion / which cannot be moved but abides forever" (Ps. 125:1). Jerusalem's physical setting also engenders a feeling of security: "The mountains are round about Jerusalem, / and the Lord is round about

---

[31] See Richard Clifford, *The Cosmic Mountain in Canaan and the Old Testament* (Cambridge: Harvard University Press, 1972), pp. 131–60.

[32] See J. J. M. Roberts, "The Davidic Origin," pp. 329–44, for a summary of the evidence and a critique of the so-called Jebusite theory of the origins of the Zion tradition.

his people" (Ps. 125:2). Jerusalem is a secure enclave, "a city firmly bound together" (Ps. 122:3). Ultimately, however, it is not the inherent nature of Zion that makes it secure but Yahweh's dwelling in the city.

> There is a river, the streams whereof make glad the city of God,
> The holiest dwelling-place of the Most High.
> God is in the midst of her; she shall not be moved [Ps. 46:5f.].

Unlike other mountains, Zion does not quiver or melt in the cosmic convulsions which accompany Yahweh's appearances as divine warrior. On the contrary, as Yahweh's residence, Mount Zion is the site from which Yahweh goes forth to defeat Israel's enemies: "The Lord of hosts will come down / to fight upon Mount Zion and upon its hill, / like birds hovering, so the Lord of hosts will protect Jerusalem" (Isa. 30:4f.). Zion becomes Yahweh's fortress, his eternal military defense post. "Within her citadels God has shown himself a sure defense" (Ps. 48:4). Zion's towers, ramparts, and citadels give sure evidence of God's eternal protection of the city (Ps. 48:13–15). Just as Yahweh protected the Israelites in the wilderness of Sinai with pillars of cloud and fire, so too will he preserve Jerusalem and its righteous. "The Lord will create over the whole site of Mount Zion and over her assemblies a cloud by day and smoke and the shining of a flaming fire by night" (Isa. 4:5). Zion is thus a refuge for the righteous, the most permanent of the mountains.

The second focus of mountain imagery, height, figures primarily, we saw, in contexts in which divine authority is at stake; height points to divinity. The attempts of foreign kings to scale the mythological mountain of God meet with disastrous results. Similarly, foreign kings cannot ascend Zion, Yahweh's chosen mountain. Only the descendant of David reigns on Zion (Ps. 2:6); foreign kings flee in fright (Ps. 48:5–7). Because Mount Zion is Yahweh's dwelling place, it becomes "beautiful in elevation" (*yĕpēh nôp*, Ps. 48:3). Despite the actual modest height of Zion, the poets transform it into a formidable peak. It even becomes identified with or replaces Baal's mountain, Zaphon, for Mount Zion is said to be located on the "extremities of Zaphon" (Ps. 48:3).

With the mountain symbol the biblical authors can express the paradox of Yahweh dwelling simultaneously in heaven and on earth. Just as a tall mountain appears to reach the sky when its peak is lost in the clouds, so too does Yahweh's dwelling place. At Mount Zion the boundary between heaven and earth is erased. Isaiah, for instance, sees "the Lord sitting upon a throne high and lifted up / and his train filled the temple" (Isa. 6:1). The adjectives, "high and lifted up" (*rām wĕniśśā'*), predicated of human arrogance, here denote the heavenly realm of Yahweh's throne. Yet, at the same time, his "train" rests in the temple. The image of the "footstool," another epithet for Mount Zion, expresses the same paradox, as this poetic parallelism makes clear:

> Exalt the Lord our God and worship at his footstool
> for he is holy . . . .
> Exalt the Lord our God and worship at his holy mountain
> for the Lord our God is holy [Ps. 99:5, 9].

Like the mountain, the footstool is an apt image to express Yahweh's sovereignty extending from heaven to earth; his throne may be in heaven, but his footstool sits on earth (cf. Isa. 66:1).

The literary convention of setting important addresses of blessing and curse on mountaintops is also applied to Mount Zion. From Mount Zion Yahweh delivers his blessing to his people:

> The Lord bless thee out of Zion
> And see then the good of Jerusalem all the days of thy life;
> And see thy children's children [Ps. 128:5f.].

More specifically, even *tôrāh* comes from Zion in Isaiah's futuristic vision (2:2f.). Furthermore, radical elevation symbolizes Zion's new authority, for Zion "shall be established as the highest of the mountains" (2:2). Ezekiel, too, envisions the new Jerusalem—not just the temple, but the entire city—set on a "very high mountain" (Ezek. 40: 2). In Zechariah's apocalyptic vision, similarly, following the final battle between Yahweh and his enemies, all the land shall be leveled but Jerusalem shall be raised (Zech. 14:10). All of these futuristic oracles show the renewed Jerusalem to be the highest mountain. Since power and authority flow from height, Jerusalem, the locus of the divine sovereignty, will soar above the land.

Third, fertility imagery also is reconfigured at Mount Zion.[33] Although fertility is a feature of the mountains in general, it is Yahweh's presence on his own chosen mountain Zion that ensures the fertility of the land. Yahweh is to be praised in Zion (Ps. 65:2) because he waters the earth and blesses its growth (vv. 10–14). Human fertility, too, results from Yahweh's blessing from Zion:

> Your wife will be like a fruitful tree within your house;
> your children will be like olive shoots around your table.
> Lo, thus shall the man be blessed who fears the Lord.
> The Lord will bless you from Zion [Ps. 128:3–6].

Mount Zion, however, has no autonomous power; when Yahweh leaves his mountain the land does not produce (Lam. 4:9). Even before the exile, Jeremiah expresses the convictions of those who say that Yahweh is "like a stranger in the land" (14:8) because there is no water or grass

---

[33] See Talmon's brief discussion in *"har; gibh'āh,"* p. 446.

(vv. 2-7). And, when after the exile the returnees find the land infertile, Haggai explains that without a house in Jerusalem, Yahweh will not bless the land. "Because of my house that lies waste and everyone of you runs to his own house. Therefore the heaven over you is restrained from giving dew, and the earth is restrained from giving its produce" (Hag. 1:9f.). Only when Yahweh dwells in Mount Zion can blessing flow to land and people.

The futuristic visions of Ezekiel and Zechariah stress the fertility that flows from the new Jerusalem just as they report its elevation. Ezekiel sees a river extending from Jerusalem to the Dead Sea, carrying life-giving water to the desert (Ezek. 47:7-12). This river, issuing from beneath the temple situated on the "very high mountain," transforms the Dead Sea into a fresh water lake and the wilderness into a lush land whose trees produce fresh fruit every month. Zechariah speaks of a similar Edenic new creation. Here, however, rivers of "living water" flow both eastward and westward from the new Jerusalem (Zech. 14:8). Furthermore, continuous day reigns (vv. 6f.) "on that day" when Yahweh reigns over all the earth (v. 9). If any "families of the earth" fail to come to Jerusalem to worship, "there will be no rain upon them" (v. 17). In the glorious future, Mount Zion thus becomes the source of extraordinary fertility and blessing.

In conclusion, although other studies have rightly emphasized that the phenomenon of "Mount Zion" should be understood within the context of the sacredness of mountains in the ancient Near East, we have examined Israel's own literary traditions as another crucial ingredient. We have seen that the mountain motif is an important component of the biblical symbol of Mount Zion and that mountain reality, in large part, stands behind the mountain motif. Israel's experience of the security, majesty, and fertility of the hills contributed both to the preservation of literary conventions which reflect these features and to the development of new applications of mountain imagery. Foremost among these developments is the depiction of Mount Zion as the most secure, the most lofty, the most blessed mountain on earth. Here, at the monarchy's foremost sacred place, mountain imagery was localized and concentrated. The sacred mountain thus exercised the biblical imagination because the mountains were an integral element of the biblical cosmos.

Chapter Four

THE SINAI SYMBOL

Although Mount Zion functioned as the signal *hieros topos* for monarchial Israel, Mount Sinai plays as crucial a role in biblical literature. On each "mountain" occurred critical events in the history of Israel, and both came to symbolize Yahweh's eternal covenant. Yet to juxtapose the two names is at once to raise questions about their respective meanings. For despite the fact that both are conceived to be "sacred mountains," they function symbolically in different ways. Mount Sinai, the source of Torah, and Mount Zion, the site of the once and future temple, represent the alpha and omega of biblical sacred geography.

Mount Sinai, like Mount Zion, was an actual place; it was not a symbol only. Yet the numinous events which tradition associates with the mountain transformed it into a wondrous and legendary peak. Moreover, because Mount Sinai lay outside the land of Canaan, the land of settlement, and thus outside of Israel's normal sphere, the real mountain receded into the hoary past. It appears, in fact, that the biblical authors did not even know its location, for only vague indications are given (Exod. 3:18; 19:1; Deut. 1:2).[1] It had become already for them a kind of mythical place of no return. Unlike "Mount Zion," a sacred symbol ultimately grounded in the profane reality of Jerusalem, Mount Sinai existed in memory only. Unlike Jerusalem, it supported neither cult nor politics. So Sinai functioned primarily as symbol for the biblical authors.

This study of the Sinai symbol has two parts. First, we explore the significance of the mountain in the narratives in which it figures prominently. Here we will outline the events and the images associated with Mount Sinai, principally those of theophany and instruction. Second, we assess the symbolic functions of Mount Sinai in the biblical tradition as a whole, by synthesizing its major symbolic valences and by noting its relationship to Mount Zion. Before proceeding, however, we must comment briefly on the nature of the Sinai traditions.

---

[1] See the discussion of M. Haran, *Ages and Institutions in the Bible* (Tel Aviv: Am Oved, 1972), pp. 48–50 (in Hebrew).

The Sinai traditions, surprisingly, occupy only a small part of biblical literature. In fact, the name "Sinai" occurs only four times outside of the Pentateuch (Judg. 5:5; Ps. 68:9,18; Neh. 9:13)! Yet "Sinai" appears to refer to three distinct geographical entities in the Bible.[2] It occurs, first of all, in the construct phrase *midbar sînay*, "wilderness of Sinai" (e.g., Exod. 19:1f.; Num. 1:1), which denotes one of the encampment stations on the wilderness journey. Second, the name designates the mountainous country south of Canaan. In several early poems, Sinai is found in concert with Seir, Edom, and Paran, indicating the arena from which Yahweh comes forth in battle against his enemies (Deut. 33:2; Judg. 5:5; Hab. 3:3–6; Ps. 68:9). Sinai here does not refer to a specific peak but rather to the southern hill region where Yahweh likely was first worshipped. Third, and most important for us, Sinai is the mountain where the newly freed slaves experience God's revelation and bind themselves to the covenant. The core of this tradition occupies Exodus 19–24, although the various legal codes and cultic instructions given at the mountain extend through much of the remainder of the Pentateuch.

In Deuteronomy and in traditions attributed to the northern Elohist and Deuteronomist, the mountain of revelation and covenant is called "Horeb." Sometimes Horeb seems to denote a general locale rather than a specific mountain (Exod. 17:6). Richard Clifford and others have noted that the Horeb traditions do not merely replicate the stories associated with Sinai.[3] The burning bush (Exod. 3–4) and golden calf (Exod. 33) episodes at "Horeb," for instance, have no counterparts at "Sinai." Whatever the original provenance of the traditions associated with the two names, the canonical Pentateuch, nonetheless, regards them as identical. Thus, at the burning bush at Horeb, Yahweh tells Moses that "when you have brought forth the people out of Egypt, you shall serve God upon this mountain" (Exod. 3:12); yet Israel is brought to Mount Sinai (Exod. 19). Similarly, in Deuteronomy, when Moses recaps the history of the wandering, he speaks of Horeb rather than Sinai (4:15). Thus, already for the biblical compilers, Sinai and Horeb were equivalents, and so subsequent tradition affirmed.[4] Although we will treat the Sinai tradition in its final, canonized form and thus sidestep the question of its origins, three influences on its development should be noted.

First, several scholars have studied the impact of Canaanite mythological understandings of revelation. F. M. Cross, for instance, has shown that the depiction of Yahweh on Mount Sinai reflects both Baal

---

[2] This three-fold division is based on the analysis of Richard Clifford, *The Cosmic Mountain*, pp. 109–20.

[3] Ibid., pp. 121–22.

[4] For instance, Sirach (48:7) praises Elijah "who heard rebuke at Sinai/ and judgments of vengeance at Horeb."

and El traditions.[5] On the one hand, Baal appears in a storm theophany as the "divine warrior," either marching to battle against his enemies or coming triumphantly to his temple on his newly-won mountain.[6] Hebrew poetry picks up this motif in the "march in the South" of Yahweh, *zeh sînay*, "the one of Sinai" (Judg. 5:5).[7] In the Sinai narrative, the motif is historicized to depict the appearance of Yahweh on the mountain of revelation. On the other hand, El characteristically reveals himself in decrees made in the council of the gods.[8] His iconographic portrait often has him sitting on a throne with his hand lifted in apparent blessing or decree. This picture resembles the view, to which Moses and the elders are privy, of Yahweh seated on his throne upon Mount Sinai giving the law (Exod. 24:10). Thus, the narrative sources appear to combine in Yahweh the images of the divine warrior, Baal, and the issuer of decrees, El. In the "march in the South" passages, however, composed well before the Sinai narrative, Cross detects only Baal imagery. Clearly, the later narrative reflects the mixing of motifs.

Second, many scholars have suggested cultic influence upon the Sinai narrative. Mowinckel asserts that the narrative originated in the liturgy of the new year celebration in Jerusalem during which the covenant was renewed.[9] More recently, Beyerlin has traced the history of a covenant renewal ceremony during the desert, early settlement, and monarchial periods, showing how cultic practice at various worship sites affected particulars of the Sinai tradition.[10] Especially at Shechem, he says, features such as the cloud of smoke representing incense, ritual consecration (Exod. 19:10), and light phenomena (Exod. 24:1,9–11) were likely to have entered the tradition. This cultic theory is appealing because it makes sense of many otherwise anomalous features of the theophany narrative. The demand for purification (Exod. 19:10), the sudden blast of the trumpet (v. 16), and the special instructions to the priests (v. 21), for instance, all fit well into a cultic ceremony but uncomfortably into a theophany story.[11]

In opposition to this theory, however, Loewenstamm insists that no evidence really exists for a connection between the Sinai narrative and any particular festival.[12] The "covenant renewal festival," which many

---

[5] Cross, *Canaanite Myth and Hebrew Epic*, pp. 185–88.

[6] Ibid., pp. 147–56.

[7] Ibid., pp. 100–103.

[8] Ibid., p. 177.

[9] Mowinckel's argument is discussed by S. Loewenstamm, "*Sinai, ma'amad har sinai*," *Encyclopedia Biblica*, vol.5, col. 1032 (in Hebrew). Mowinckel's classic study of the subject is *Le Décalogue*, Etudes d'histoire et de philosophie religieuses, no. 16 (Paris: Felix Alcan, 1927).

[10] Walter Beyerlin, *Origins and History of the Oldest Sinaitic Traditions*, trans. S. Rudman (Oxford: Basil Blackwell, 1965), pp. 145–67.

[11] The priesthood had not yet been instituted according to the narrative (cf. Exod. 24:5).

[12] Loewenstamm, "*Sinai*," col. 1032.

scholars infer, does not appear on any of the cultic calendars. The feast of Weeks, *Shabuot*, which later came to celebrate the giving of the Torah, is never associated with the Sinai covenant in the Bible. But, although there may be no single festival for which the Sinai narrative or its sources served as a liturgy, it seems likely that the cult has influenced the shape of the tradition.

Third, von Rad has claimed that the Sinai tradition, as a whole, was originally separate from the "exodus" and "wandering" traditions and was connected to it only by the so-called Yahwist. Von Rad takes his cue from the fact that, although the Sinai events are the focus of the Pentateuch, they are ignored in several creedal formulations (e.g., Deut. 26:5–9; 6:20–24; Josh. 24:2b–13) and in lyrical adaptations of them (e.g., Pss. 136; 105; Exod. 15).[13] Accepting Mowinckel's view of the cultic origin of the Sinai tradition, he proposes a *Sitz im Leben* in a covenant renewal festival at Shechem connected with the feast of Booths. Against von Rad's theory, Herbert Huffmon, among others, has urged that Sinai was not a saving event like those recalled in the creeds and, thus, that its absence there is not surprising.[14] The creed, rather, is analogous to the historical prologue of the Hittite covenant treaties and details the gracious acts of the sovereign on which the Sinai covenant is based. If Huffmon is correct, the canonical connection between "exodus" and Sinai reflects an original link in the tradition rather than a secondary connection. In any case, this link is integral to the canonical sacred history and, therefore, to the meaning of the Sinai symbol itself.

Images in the Narratives

With this awareness of the checkered history of the Sinai tradition in mind, we proceed to examine the narratives in which the mountain Sinai-Horeb is accorded a major role. The mountain is the site of three events in biblical sacred history. First, in the episode of the burning bush (Exod. 3–4), Yahweh confronts Moses. Second, in the focus of the Pentateuch, the covenant is offered, specified, and concluded (Exod. 19–24). The legal codes attached to the covenant then extend through most of Exodus, Leviticus, and Numbers, and the Deuteronomist has Moses recount the covenant making (e.g., Deut. 4:9–14) and summarize the law. Third, after fleeing from Samaria, the prophet Elijah finds Yahweh at Horeb. His journey represents the first and last return to the mountain after the time of Moses (1 Kings 19). In each of these stories, Yahweh comes in a marvelous way in order to issue a critically important commission: he appears in the burning bush to enlist Moses

---

[13] von Rad, *The Problem of the Hexateuch and Other Essays*, pp. 1–13.
[14] Herbert Huffmon, "The Exodus, Sinai, and the Credo," pp. 101–13.

as leader of the exodus; he reveals his will amid a violent storm and offers Israel his laws; and his voice echoes sublimely in the ear of Elijah who is recommissioned in the battle against Baal. Theophany and instruction thus mark off the mountain as distinct, wholly other, sacred. Now let us look specifically at the images in these stories through which the biblical authors express their understanding of the significance of this sacred mountain.

Moses at the Bush

The sacred mountain first enters the narrative abruptly in the story of the burning bush. Leading his flocks deep into the wilderness (*'aḥar hammidbār*), Moses "came to the mountain of God (*har hā'elohîm*), to Horeb" (Exod. 3:1). The author conveys Moses' complete surprise at the encounter. "That it was the mountain of God is made out to be as little known to Moses as Bethel's being the 'gate of heaven' was known to Jacob."[15] Yet the definite article denominates both mountain and bush as if they were known previously.[16] This denomination, however, may be proleptic: this is "the" mountain that would become Yahweh's mountain.[17] In any case, the mountain has no previous history in the Bible and here is given no geographical coordinates; Moses simply chances upon it.

At the burning bush Yahweh appears, classically, as *mysterium tremendum et fascinans*.[18] Suddenly Moses finds himself in the presence of *mysterium*: a bush which burns but is not consumed. What he sees cannot be subsumed within nature; it is unnatural, uncanny, numinous. Drawn to explore it further, Moses turns from his path and approaches; Yahweh is *fascinans*. And then Yahweh calls to him, warning him to stop and remove his shoes before the holy ground; Yahweh is *tremendum*. The dialogue that ensues between Yahweh and Moses reflects the opposing forces of fear and fascination at the heart of the religious experience. Moses is caught in Yahweh's grip; he struggles unsuccessfully to extricate himself from the task demanded of him. At the same time, he is drawn inexorably into the divine conspiracy and emerges as Yahweh's confederate.

This theophany is thus intended not simply to surprise or to confirm a promise, as in the case of Jacob's dream at Bethel (Gen. 28:10–17); it rather issues in instruction. The voice at the burning bush commissions

---

[15] Moshe Greenberg, *Understanding Exodus* (New York: Behrman, 1969), p.68.

[16] Martin Buber, *Moses: The Revelation and the Covenant* (New York: Harper and Row, 1958), p. 39.

[17] U. Cassuto, *A Commentary on the Book of Exodus*, trans. I. Abrahams (Jerusalem: Magnes, 1967), p. 31.

[18] See Rudolph Otto, *The Idea of the Holy*, trans. J. W. Harvey (London: Oxford University Press, 1958), pp. 12–40.

Moses to be Yahweh's messenger to Pharaoh, his agent in the over-throw of the forces of oppression and the liberation of the Hebrews. Moses arrives at Horeb as a shepherd and departs as the spokesman for Yahweh. From the mountain outside of Egypt, God issues the charge to Moses to reenter the Egypt which he fled. In this episode, then, Horeb enters the religious imagination as the site where, in the midst of a bush, Yahweh appeared uniquely to Moses. There Yahweh first reveals his name and his intentions for Israel. There he initiates the course of events which will bring the entire people back to him at the mountain. Horeb is thus Yahweh's home base from which he ventures forth to empower Moses in Egypt but to which he returns to greet his people in the second narrative.

Israel at Sinai

The second episode at the mountain follows from the first. Yahweh, as we noted, had told Moses at the bush that he would return with his people to "this mountain" (Exod. 3:12). Although the tradition here calls the mountain Sinai rather than Horeb, the author clearly sees Israel's arrival at the mountain to fulfill Yahweh's promise. In fact, the first theophany prefigures this one in several respects. The fire of the bush, for instance, anticipates the fiery appearance of Yahweh on Sinai (Exod. 19:18). Indeed, before Moses the bush "was not consumed" and before Israel Yahweh appears atop the mountain as a "consuming fire" (Exod. 24:17; Deut. 4:24). In both, the holiness of the ground is stressed. Just as Moses removes his shoes before the bush (Exod. 3:5), so the people must purify themselves (Exod. 19:10) and refrain from touching the mountain (v. 12). In the second narrative, several motifs conjoin to depict a dramatic and intense theophany. At Sinai, Yahweh manifests himself in the storm as the divine warrior. At the same time, the cloud that accompanies him appears to symbolize divine kingship. Furthermore, on the mountain Yahweh is uniquely visible. Finally, the theophany issues in the giving of the law. These four motifs require individual treatment.

First, a violent storm heralds the descent of Yahweh upon Mount Sinai. Yahweh appears amid "thunders, lightnings, and a thick cloud upon the mountain," and the mountain quakes and smokes as the trumpet blows and God speaks in thunder (Exod. 19:16,19). While Noth believes that the description is of a volcano and therefore locates Mount Sinai in the Arabian peninsula where volcanoes were to be found, Cross cautions against "send[ing] for seismologists."[19] He notes that during thunder storms, when lightning strikes trees near the timber line of high mountains, fire and smoke are emitted. Thus violent thunderstorms likely stand behind the storm imagery.

---

[19] Cross, *Canaanite Myth*, p. 169.

As we remarked above, whatever the specific source of the imagery, it had come to be associated with the Canaanite storm god Baal and then with Yahweh when he appeared as "divine warrior." In fact, as Loewenstamm points out, earth tremors regularly accompany the theophanies of military gods in Akkadian sources as well: Marduk, Enlil, Adad, Ishtar.[20] But Shamash, the god of judgment and law, he notes, causes no earth quaking. Similarly, the Canaanite El, a more passive god, issues decrees, not thunder. Although at Sinai Yahweh is preeminently a god of law like El, he is nonetheless seen also as the divine warrior. Here, as elsewhere, he combines functions divided among the gods in other ancient Near Eastern systems.

The storm imagery, indeed, forms part of a wider military motif in the narrative. The description of the Sinai event exhibits four features of the institution of "holy war": consultation with the deity, consecration of the army, blowing of the trumpet, proclamation of ḥerem, ban, against the enemy.[21] First, Moses consults with Yahweh upon arriving at the mountain (19:3) and then declares his will to the people. Second, the "people" (i.e., the males) are consecrated (v. 14). While, of course, the injunction to consecration precedes other cultic undertakings, it is mentioned most often in connection with "holy war" (1 Sam. 21:6; 2 Sam. 11:11). Third, the anomalous blowing of the trumpet precedes the proclamation of the Decalogue (v. 19). Finally, the announcement of ḥerem against the inhabitants of Canaan concludes the Covenant Code (23:23f.). These features, adapted from the imagery of holy war, suggest that Mount Sinai is conceived to be Yahweh's "headquarters" from which he will lead his people into his land.[22]

A second image associated with Yahweh's appearance on the mountain is the cloud (ʿānān). The cloud, which covers the mountain during the theophany (Exod. 19:9,16) and envelops Moses throughout his forty

---

[20] S. Loewenstamm, "Raʿadat haṭṭevaʿ bēšaʿat hôpāʿat haššēm," ʿOz ledavid (Jerusalem: Kiryat Sepher, 1964), pp. 508–509 (in Hebrew).

[21] These features of "holy war" are analyzed by G. von Rad, *Studies in Deuteronomy*, trans. D. Stalker, Studies in Biblical Theology, no. 9 (London: SCM Press, 1953), pp. 47–48. His classic study of the subject is *Der Heilige Krieg im Alten Israel* (Göttingen: Vandenhoeck and Ruprecht, 1958).

[22] In fact, the entire journey from Egypt to Canaan has the character of a military expedition. Yahweh first appears as "man of war" at the Red Sea (Exod. 15:3) where his wind pushes the sea over the Egyptians (v. 10). In the prose version (Exod. 14), Moses exhorts the people with typical "holy war" language: "Fear not, stand firm . . . The Lord will fight for you" (vv. 13f.; cf. Josh. 8:1; 10:25). On the journey Yahweh first battles Amalek (Exod. 17), later the Midianites, and eventually the inhabitants of Canaan. Furthermore, the attention given to the organization of the camps, the tribal standards, and the order of march (e.g., Num. 10) suggest a military march. Even the kind of encampment itinerary detailed in Num. 33:1–49 has parallels in ancient Near Eastern royal military campaigns. See G. I. Davies, "The Wilderness Itineraries: A Comparative Study," *Tyndale Bulletin* 25 (1974): 48–61.

days and nights atop the peak, serves several symbolic functions (Exod. 24:18). It is, to begin with, an element of the storm imagery which expresses Yahweh's control of nature and his military might. Like Baal, whose epithet is "rider of the clouds" (*rkb 'rpt*), Yahweh as divine warrior appears surrounded by "bright cloud (*'ānān*) and storm cloud (*'arāpel*)" (Ps. 97:2; cf. Ps. 18:13).[23] The cloud, however, appears independently of the storm theophany and must, therefore, have other connotations as well. As the "pillar of cloud" (*'ammûd 'ānān*), for instance, it serves in tandem with the "pillar of fire" (*'ammûd 'ēš*) and accompanies the Hebrews from the border of Egypt (Exod. 13:21) to the border of Canaan (Deut. 31:15).[24] The cloud also descends upon the tent of meeting when Moses enters to speak with God, or, as another text has it, the cloud by day and the fire by night rest upon the tent to prevent Moses from entering. Only when it ascends do the Israelites journey onward (Exod. 40: 34–38; Num. 10:11f.).

In these cases, the *'ānān* functions as an image of divine sovereignty. The pillar of cloud that leads the Hebrews through the wilderness expresses the divine guidance. Through the *'ānān*, Yahweh overwhelms the Egyptian armies at the sea and shows his sovereign power over the Hebrews at the mountain. Similarly, the pillar of cloud upon the tent inspires awe before the divine power: "And when all the people saw the pillar of cloud standing at the door of the tent, all the people would rise up and worship, every man at his tent door" (Exod. 33:10). George Mendenhall, interestingly, identifies the biblical *'ānān* to be the equivalent of the Akkadian *melammû*, the nimbus surrounding the divine which conceals its body. Represented iconographically as a winged sun disk, the *melammû* was "a universal symbol of sovereignty in the ancient world."[25] The description of the Sinai theophany, says Mendenhall, employs the *melammû* symbolism, but was written by someone who did not fully understand it.

The cloud further serves as an image of concealment. When the Egyptians pursue, the pillar of cloud moves to a rearward position in order to hide the Hebrews from them. In the tent, the pillar of cloud denies the people access to Yahweh while Moses enters to speak to Yahweh within (Exod. 33:9). Most dramatically, during the Sinai theophany, the cloud conceals the essence of Yahweh from the people at the same time that it reveals his presence. After the Decalogue is proclaimed, "the people stood afar off, while Moses drew near to the thick

---

[23] At Mount Sinai, as elsewhere, the *'ānān* (Exod. 19:9, *'ab he 'ānān*) is not clearly differentiated from the *'arāpel*, "thick cloud" (20:21) or the *kābôd*, "glory" (24:16). See Cross, *Canaanite Myth*, p. 166.

[24] Originally the two pillars were probably one, the "pillar of fire and cloud" (Exod. 14:24). See the remarks of George Mendenhall, *The Tenth Generation*, p. 58.

[25] Mendenhall, *The Tenth Generation*, pp. 61–66. But see Cross's criticism in *Canaanite Myth*, pp. 165–66, n. 86.

cloud (*'arāpel*) where God was" (Exod. 20:20). After the covenant is ratified, only Moses enters the cloud; to the people Yahweh still appears as a devouring fire (Exod. 24:15–17). On the mountain, then, Yahweh displays his sovereignty yet conceals himself with the *'ānān*.

A third important motif which distinguishes Mount Sinai from all other places is the direct vision of Yahweh experienced there. At Sinai, while the cloud conceals him from the many, the mountain provides access to him for the few. When Moses, Aaron, Nadab, Abihu, and the seventy elders ascend the mountain after the ratification of the covenant, "they saw (*wayyir'û*) the God of Israel . . . . And he did not lay his hand on the chief men of the people of Israel; they beheld (*wayyeḥezû*) God, and ate and drank" (Exod. 24:10f.). This statement, unique in the Bible, sounds all the more remarkable following, as it does, the theophany where great precautions are taken to block the people's vision of Yahweh. The verb "beheld" (*ḥāzāh*) connotes especially intense seeing with the eyes or the intelligence (cf. Ps. 11:7; 17:14; 63:3) and is used of a seer in ecstasy.[26] Because it occurs almost almost exclusively in poetry, its unusual employment here underscores the uniqueness of the event. Nicholson believes that Exod. 24:9–11 originally had nothing to do with the covenant but rather represents a separate and very old theophany tradition which knows nothing of the hiddenness of Yahweh, the storm phenomena, or Moses as mediator.[27] Its purpose was solely to depict the vision of Yahweh atop Mount Sinai.

The image of Yahweh's throne is central to this vision, for the author describes not Yahweh himself but his throne room. "There was under his feet as it were a pavement of sapphire stone, like the very heaven for clearness" (Exod. 24:10). This image may derive from ancient Near Eastern royal use of lapis lazuli or simply from the blueness of the sky. In fact, Baal's palace on Mount Zaphon is said to be bricked with this blue stone.[28] Before this sight, the elders "ate and drank," rejoicing in Yahweh's presence (cf. Exod. 18:12; Deut. 12:7; 14:26).[29] The throne also appears in Isaiah's vision in the temple (Isa. 6:1) and in Ezekiel's vision of the chariot (Ezek. 1:26; 10:1). In both cases, the throne is connected with Mount Zion where, similarly, the "mountain" facilitates the vision of God's dwelling place.

The climactic vision of Yahweh belongs to Moses uniquely. He alone enters the cloud and remains with Yahweh twice for forty days

---

[26] Francis Brown, S. R. Driver, and C. A. Briggs, *A Hebrew and English Lexicon of the Old Testament* (London: Oxford University Press, 1907), p. 302.

[27] E. W. Nicholson, "The Interpretation of Ex. 24:9–11," *Vetus Testamentum* 24 (1974): 94–97.

[28] Clifford, *The Cosmic Mountain*, p. 112.

[29] Nicholson notes that eating and drinking are not necessarily associated with a covenant meal. In this case eating and drinking accompany a theophany, not a covenant ceremony ("The Interpretation of Ex. 24:9–11," p. 93).

and nights (Exod. 24:18; 34:28). When he descends, the numinous glow from his face witnesses to his special vision of the divine (34:29–35). Furthermore, in the tent of meeting, "the Lord used to speak to Moses face to face (pānîm 'el-pānîm), as a man speaks to his friend" (33:11). Yet another text has Yahweh respond to Moses' request to see his glory: "you cannot see my face (pānâ); for man shall not see me and live. . . .You shall see my back ('aḥorâ); but my face shall not be seen" (33:20,23; cf. Gen. 32:30). Although these contradictory texts would seem to derive from different sources, their juxtaposition serves to emphasize that on the mountain Yahweh reveals to Moses what he has revealed to no one else (Exod. 34:3).

The divine warrior in the storm, the sovereign and hidden god in the cloud, the king on his throne who yet speaks to Moses face to face — these images intersect to express the significance and the sacredness of the place which Yahweh has chosen to reveal his will to his people. They create a richly numinous backdrop for the giving of the law, the event for which Mount Sinai is most renowned. At Mount Sinai, Yahweh commissions his people by setting before them laws which are the stipulations of a covenant treaty. In this, his only public address to Israel, Yahweh proclaims those laws which are to bind the fugitive Hebrews into a special (sĕgullāh, Exod. 19:5; Deut. 14:2) people.

Beginning with the Decalogue, "the preliminary statement of principles, which forms the preamble to the covenant proper,"[30] and continuing with the "Covenant Code," a rather miscellaneous collection of casuistic law, the Pentateuch weaves the law into the Sinai story. Although subsequent collections incorporated into the Pentateuch impede the progress of the story, they testify to the continued claim that from the mountain all law proceeds. The law, the social and religious order, does not grow with or in society; it is anterior to and outside of it. Not only are the laws transmitted and written "with the finger of God" (Exod. 31:18) on Mount Sinai, but there too the plans for the priestly sancta can be directly viewed. "According to all that I show you concerning the pattern (tabnît) of the tabernacle, and of all its furniture, so shall you make it. . . . And see that you make them after the pattern for them (bĕtabnîtām), which is being shown you on the mountain" (Exod. 25:9, 40). These two verses, which frame the instructions for the ark, table, and lampstand make it clear that Moses sees on the mountain the plans for the construction.[31] In short, Mount Sinai is the

---

[30] Cassuto, Commentary on Exodus, p. 240.

[31] R. G. Hamerton-Kelly, "The Temple and the Origins of Jewish Apocalyptic" Vetus Testamentum 20 (1970): 5–6, argues that tabnît refers to a pre-existent heavenly prototype which Moses sees and is commanded to copy. Yet in our text the word tabnît appears to be equivalent to the word mišpāṭ, "rule." "And you shall erect the tabernacle according to its rule (kĕmišpāṭô) which has been shown you on the mountain" (Exod. 26:30). Similarly,

place where the divine plan is communicated and transmitted to the human world.

Elijah at Horeb

The final episode to occur at the sacred mountain centers upon Elijah, the only person who returns to Horeb. The story of Elijah evokes many earlier images, for it aims to sketch a portrait of Elijah as the "prophet like Moses."[32] At Horeb, Elijah, like Moses, has a private audience with Yahweh. Like Moses, who neither eats nor drinks for forty days upon the mountain (Exod. 34:28), Elijah fasts for forty days on his journey to Horeb. Like Moses, Elijah stands upon ('āmad, 1 Kings 19:11; Deut. 10:10) the mountain and Yahweh passes by ('ābar, 1 Kings 19:11; Exod. 33:22). Here, too, Yahweh comes in the storm represented by wind, earthquake, and fire. Yet here, in a new twist, following the storm comes the mysterious "voice," the qôl demāmāh daqqāh, which echoes eerily on the mountain. Beautifully, the author thus claims that Yahweh is behind, not within, the meteorological pyrotechnics. Whether the intent is a "still small voice" or a "roaring and thunderous voice," clearly, at Horeb, Yahweh confers upon Elijah a presence which only Moses before him had experienced.[33]

Elijah goes to Horeb because it is the "mountain of God" (1 Kings 19:8), and he wants to confront Yahweh directly. The "word of Yahweh" which pulses through the Elijah cycle of stories had commissioned Elijah in the battle against Baal. But now, pursued by Jezebel, Elijah feels that the battle is lost, so he flees to Yahweh's "home turf" to resign his post.[34] Escaping the wrath of Jezebel, he takes refuge in Yahweh's mountain, but the word of the Lord greets him with the question, "What are you doing *here*, Elijah?" (19:9). Why have you abandoned your post? Elijah replies, "The people of Israel have forsaken thy covenant. . . and I, even I only, am left, and they seek my life, to take it away" (19:10,14). Elijah believes that the covenant is irredeemably broken, that Baal will triumph.

The theophany, then, in response to Elijah's plaint is a statement that Elijah is wrong, that the covenant is still in force, that Yahweh is still in control. At Horeb the covenant is reconfirmed. The "voice"

---

in 1 Chron. 28:11 David gives Solomon the *tabnît* for the temple. Here the *tabnît* is clearly the writing (v. 19) of the plan for the building, not a scale model.

[32] R. A. Carlson, "Elie a L'Horeb," *Vetus Testamentum* 19 (1969): 416–39.

[33] J. Lust, on the basis of philological analyses of the words *demāmāh* and *daqqāh*, concludes that the "voice" is not meant as a contrast to the theopany but as the "roaring and thunderous voice" which proceeds from it. "A Gentle Breeze or a Roaring Thunderous Sound," *Vetus Testamentum* 25 (1975): 110–15.

[34] This interpretation follow E. von Nordheim, "Ein Prophet kündigt sein Amt auf (Elia am Horeb)," *Biblica* 59 (1978): 153–73, esp. 160–67.

sends him back to Samaria to gather new warriors to take up the gauntlet against the followers of Baal. Elijah must return to the political arena to anoint new kings in Israel and even in Baalist Aram and to appoint a new prophet to replace himself. Although Yahweh seems to accept Elijah's resignation, he insists that, like Plato's philosopher, Elijah must leave the cave and return to society.

The Elijah episode confirms the basic conception of the mountain represented in earlier episodes. Horeb is seen to be Yahweh's home. In fact, the author may well intend to convey Yahweh's anger at Elijah for approaching the sacred precinct uninvited. Here Yahweh again manifests himself in the storm as the divine warrior and treats his prophet to a special vision. Here, too, the Sinai covenant is reaffirmed, and the theophany issues in instruction to implement the covenant.

Functions of the Symbol

Symbolic Valences

After surveying the images of theophany and instruction associated with Mount Sinai in the three narratives in which it figures prominently, we can view synoptically the symbolic functions of the mountain in the biblical imagination. What makes this "sacred mountain" distinctive? Three symbolic valences emerge from the stories to locate the mountain in sacred space and time. First, within the Pentateuch, Sinai is the preeminent *axis mundi*. Simultaneously, on the horizontal axis, it functions as a peripheral pivot. Finally, temporally, Sinai is linked to the beginnings of Israel, for it represents the *illud tempus*, the primal time.

To begin with, as *har hā'elohîm*, the "mountain of God," Mount Sinai is an *axis mundi*, a link between heaven and earth. Reaching up into the clouds, the mountain, for the ancients, was often associated with divinity, for it seemed to connect heavenly and earthly realms. The biblical texts, as we have seen, do not present a uniform picture of just how Yahweh is connected to the mountain. On the one hand, the stories of Moses (Exod. 3–4) and Elijah (1 Kings 19) seem to assume that Yahweh resided permanently at the mountain. To the mountain Moses is to return and to the mountain Elijah flees to confront Yahweh directly. Similarly, when Moses brings the Hebrews back to Sinai, "Moses went up to God" (Exod. 19:3); that is where Yahweh was to be found. Yet the texts relating the great theophany suggest that Yahweh descends upon the mountain only for this one occasion (Exod. 19–20). Furthermore, although some texts have Yahweh speak from the mountain (Exod. 19:20), the latest text confusingly relates: "Thou didst come down upon the mountain and speak with them from heaven" (Neh. 9:13).

These various texts together express the paradox of the transcendent becoming immanent, the omnipresent becoming localized. In the compact symbols of the bush, the cloud, and the "still small voice" this paradox is crystallized. In the bush which burns but is not consumed an angel appears, but Yahweh speaks. In the cloud the power of Yahweh is signified, but the face of Yahweh is hidden. In the voice the will of Yahweh is heard—but beyond, not within, nature's fury. At the mountain divine law is transformed into human law and a society is forged. At the *axis mundi* Yahweh and Israel meet and then go forth as partners.

If the term *axis mundi* captures the vertical symbolism of Mount Sinai, then the idea of the "peripheral pivot" expresses its horizontal symbolism. Unlike many "sacred mountains" in the history of religions, Mount Sinai was not regarded as a mid-point, a geographical center. Kadesh rather than Sinai is used as a point of orientation, a base camp, during the wilderness period (e.g., Num. 13:26; 20:1). The mountain is remote, far from civilization, in the uncharted wilderness. It is connected neither to the fathers of Israel nor to Egyptian civilization. It is thus free of both patriarchal attachment and pagan taint.

In his morphological study of pilgrimage centers, Victor Turner discusses a contrast that may illuminate a symbolic function of a peripheral pivot.[35] He notes that in west and central Africa there are two types of shrines. The first is the ancestral or political shrine which represents selfish and sectional interests and stresses exclusiveness and local history. These shrines are localized churches and temples. The other type is the earth or fertility cult which represents bonds between groups and stresses disinterestedness, shared values, guilt, and responsibility of all. Its shrines are pilgrim centers which are generally located not in city centers but on their perimeters or outside them entirely. The pilgrimage process stresses going "out there" to be transformed and then returning as a new person.

Whether or not Mount Sinai was historically a pilgrim oasis (and there is some evidence that it might have been),[36] it functions symbolically in a way similar to pilgrimage shrines of the African systems. Mount Sinai acts as a kind of earth shrine, a mountain which can be understood as a concentration of earth's forces.[37] "All Israel" comes to Sinai and is bound together by values and responsibilities to be shared. The journey to the mountain transforms the fugitive Hebrews into the people of Israel. Jerusalem, by contrast, fits more into the model of the

[35] Turner, "The Center Out There: Pilgrim's Goal," p. 207.

[36] Num. 33:1–37; Deut. 1:2. This idea is defended by M. Noth, "Der Wallfahrtsweg zum Sinai (Num. 33)," *Palästinajahrbuch* 36 (1940): 5–28.

[37] This interpretation of the sacrality of the mountain is discussed by H. G. Quaritch-Wales, *The Mountain of God: A Study in Early Religion and Kingship* (London: Bernard Quaritch, 1953), p. 115.

political shrine, for it is a royal city which represents the regional interests of Judah and the factional interests of the Davidic house. Its temple is crown property open only to those with the right credentials. The incipient rivalry between Sinai and Zion, discussed below, may reflect something of the conflict between a royal shrine and one claiming older and broader allegiance.

As a peripheral pivot, then, Mount Sinai is a sacred place to which people journey and from which they return transformed. Moses happens upon the mountain as a shepherd and becomes Yahweh's messenger. He returns to Midian (Exod. 4:18) and thence to Egypt (4:20) whence he first came. He becomes a new man whose sense of identity with his people has been illuminated in the glow of the burning bush. The Hebrews come to the mountain along with a "mixed multitude" newly freed from slavery. At the mountain they are bound into one people, and they journey onward to Canaan where their fathers had been sojourners. Freed from the bondage of Egypt, they are, at Sinai, bound to the freedom of Yahweh. Elijah, lastly, treks to the mountain to plead for death, but at the pivot he is turned around, given a new task.

Finally, the sacred mountain is the beginning of time for the people of Israel, the take-off point for Israelite history. All that precedes it is preparatory. The forging of a people from the seed of Abraham occurs only at Sinai. There Yahweh covenants with the people who will be his *gôy qādôš*, his separate people, chosen from among all the peoples spun off in the tables of nations. Although "all the earth is mine" (Exod. 19:5), Israel alone is *'ammî*, "my people," by virtue of the law which it receives at Sinai. The law is Israel's alone and is Israel's *raison d'être*. As the mountain of the beginning, Sinai is thus preeminently the mountain of law. The law descends from heaven at the mountain and sets the directions for the embryonic people. With law in hand, Israel marches on to the promised land. It emerges from Sinai responsible for adherence to the covenant and suffers heavy punishments in the wilderness when it complains of its fate. Law is thus conceived to be "in the beginning," not created by society but itself creating society. The retrojection of various later law codes to Sinai indicates the pervasive hold of this concept of law on the biblical mind.

Mount Sinai represents the beginning of time because there creation occurs, the creation of Israel. Indeed, the giving of the law at Sinai is analogous to the act of bringing order out of chaos in creation myths. In Egypt, the Hebrews were like "an infinitely fertile womb," multiplying, but without direction.[38] From the midst of the multiplication Moses arises and Yahweh commissions him to deliver his "first-born son" (Exod. 4:22f.) from the oppression.[39] The plagues gradually discriminate

---

[38] See Greenberg's excellent reading in *Understanding Exodus*, pp. 57-60.

[39] See Eric Voegelin's interesting interpretation of this phrase: *Israel and Revelation*, pp. 388-95.

between the Hebrews and their Egyptian hosts until, at last, out of the chaos of destruction, the Hebrews emerge. But they are not yet fully born. They are free of Egypt but not yet free for a purpose, as their murmuring immediately makes clear. But then at Sinai the vertical descent of Yahweh interrupts the horizontal movement of escape and creates a people of purpose from the fugitive slaves. Indeed, Israel always retained its self-conscious memory of being a created, a covenanted, not a "natural" people. It remembered its creation at Mount Sinai.

Symbolic Afterlife

Axis mundi, peripheral pivot, beginning point—these three symbolic functions describe the shape of the Sinai symbol in the stories in which it figures. But, as we noted at the outset, Mount Sinai is rarely mentioned outside of the Pentateuch. As the mountain of the past, it appears to have played little active role in the life of monarchial Israel. Sinai and its covenant gave way to the holy mountain Zion and the covenant with the house of David in the official religion of the state. Nonetheless, Sinai makes itself felt in subtle ways in royalist literature. Moreover, the canonization of the Pentateuch forces Sinai and Zion into literary relationship with each other as successive, seminal, sacred mountains. Post-biblical writings pick up and develop this relationship. To complete this picture of the Sinai symbol, then, we must glance briefly at its "afterlife" in relation to Mount Zion.

Just as Mount Zion absorbs mountain imagery in general, so too does it take on motifs connected with Mount Sinai. The royalist writers, who claimed that Yahweh had come to dwell in Jerusalem, sought to make that claim continuous with the older traditions of Yahweh's dwelling in the south, particularly on Mount Sinai. As David dramatized Jerusalem's claim to be the successor to the ancient tribal centers by bringing the ark up to his city, so too the royalist writers incorporated Sinai imagery into their descriptions of Mount Zion.[40] In so doing, they said implicitly, at least, that the God of Sinai, *zeh sînay*, was now accessible in Jerusalem.

Several of the images of the Sinai theophany recur at Jerusalem-Mount Zion. The most prominent is that of Yahweh as divine warrior who comes in the storm and makes nature convulse. This imagery, which, as we saw earlier, is a stereotypic way of representing Yahweh's appearance, probably developed from a tradition about Yahweh's march in the southern hill country which was localized first at Mount Sinai and

---

[40] It is probably also true that the final form of the Sinai tradition was influenced by cultic practice at Jerusalem; i.e., the influence was likely mutual.

then transferred to Mount Zion.[41] Isaiah, especially, employs this language when he writes of Yahweh's battles against both his wayward people (28:1f.) and the nations (29:5–8):

> And in an instant, suddenly,
>   you will be visited by the Lord of hosts
> with thunder and with earthquake and great noise
> with whirlwind and tempest and the flame of a devouring fire.

The "devouring fire" characteristic both of the burning bush and of Yahweh's appearance on Sinai will come to Zion. In another futuristic scene, the cloud also appears: Yahweh will "create over the whole site of Mount Zion and over her assemblies a cloud (*'ānān*) by day and smoke and the shining of a flaming fire by night" (Isa. 4:5). In fact, when Solomon dedicates the temple, the Deuteronomist relates that "the cloud filled the house of the Lord" (1 Kings 8:10). The cloud, which represents Yahweh's sovereignty and protection, settles in Jerusalem in Yahweh's permanent house.

The image of the direct vision of Yahweh on the mountain is also associated with Jerusalem. In the temple the boundary between heaven and earth becomes transparent; there Isaiah "saw the Lord sitting upon a throne, high and lifted up" (6:1). Yet Isaiah describes not Yahweh but the seraphim around him. Ezekiel, in his spectacular vision of the chariot over Jerusalem, sees atop the chariot "the likeness of a throne, its appearance like sapphire" (1:26) as did the elders above Sinai (Exod. 24:9). Similarity of imagery ("a great cloud, a flashing fire," 1:4; cf. Exod. 19:16,18) and circumlocutory language ("the *appearance* of the glory of the Lord," 1:28; cf. Exod. 24:17) in Ezekiel and the Pentateuchal (priestly) narrative suggest direct literary relationship.[42] Both refrain from describing Yahweh himself, although on the temple mount in Jerusalem, as at Sinai, the window to heaven is open.

In a few biblical passages it would appear not only that Mount Zion has absorbed Sinai imagery but also that Mount Zion has become a kind of rival or successor to Mount Sinai. For instance, in the famous futuristic oracle of Isaiah (2:2–4; cf. Mic. 4:1–3), the nations stream to Mount Zion, now the highest mountain, to hear the instruction once given to Israel alone on Mount Sinai. "For out of Zion shall go forth *tôrāh*, and the word of the Lord from Jerusalem." Sinai is not mentioned here, but Zion fulfills its role. Again, in the more difficult Psalm 68, Mount Zion claims superiority over the other mountains:

---

[41] Clifford, *The Cosmic Mountain*, pp. 114–20.
[42] For a study of the literary parallels see Millar Burrows, *The Literary Relations of Ezekiel* (Philadelphia: Jewish Publication Society, 1925), pp. 47–67, esp. pp. 57–58.

> A mountain of God is the mountain of Bashan;
> A high mountain is the mountain of Bashan.
> Why do you look askance you high mountains
> At the mountain which God hath desired for his abode?
> Yea, the Lord will dwell in it forever [vv. 16–17].

Is Mount Sinai among the rejected mountains? It does seem that the focus of the psalm, if it is understood as a unit, shifts from Sinai (vv. 9, 17) to Zion (vv. 25, 30, 36).[43] One emendation of v. 18 yields: "The Lord came from Sinai into the holy place" (*baqqodeš*, cf. v. 25).[44] This reading supports the idea that the poem celebrates Yahweh's victory march from Sinai to Mount Zion. Zion, then, has replaced Sinai as the divine abode.

Despite these hints, the two sacred mountains are never juxtaposed in the Hebrew Bible. Later writings, however, perceiving the thrust of biblical sacred geography, bring them into direct relationship. For the author of Jubilees, for instance, the Garden of Eden, the Mount of the East, Mount Sinai, and Mount Zion are God's four places on the earth (4:26). Mount Sinai is "the mountain on which thou art today," and Mount Zion "will be sanctified in the new creation for a sanctification of the earth." With the Garden of Eden, these two holy centers are allotted to the territory of Shem, the ancestors of the Hebrews. The author has thus identified the two mountains as the two geographical loci of Israel.

In 2 Esdras, Ezra, fashioned into a second Moses, hears God's word on Mount Horeb (2:33) and then sees a vision of the saviour on Mount Zion (2:42ff., a Christian prologue). Further, in his recall of sacred history, Ezra says that God led Israel to Mount Sinai and gave it a "commandment" (3:17–19). But Israel was overcome with sin until God chose David and "commanded him to build a city for thy name" (v. 24). The commandment to David follows directly upon the failure of the commandment at Sinai. A similar telescoping of history occurs in Acts 7. Here Stephen asserts that despite the "living oracles" (v. 38) and the tent of witness which Moses had given to Israel at Mount Sinai, the people disobeyed and David wanted to build God a house (vv. 44–47). But God "does not dwell in houses made with hands" (v. 48).

---

[43] The debate over the meaning of this psalm is still vigorous. W. F. Albright claimed that the psalm was a catalogue of incipits, first lines of poems: "A Catalogue of Early Hebrew Lyric Poems," *Hebrew Union College Annual* 23 (1950–51): 1–39. Mowinckel argued against Albright that Ps. 68 is a perfect unity belonging to the enthronement festival of Yahweh. For a discussion of the issues see P. D. Miller, *The Divine Warrior in Early Israel* (Cambridge, Mass.: Harvard University Press, 1973), p. 103.

[44] S. Talmon reads and interprets the passage this way in "The Biblical Concept of Jerusalem," *Journal of Ecumenical Studies* 8 (1971): 308. However, there are many other readings: A. Weiser: "the Lord is with them, Sinai is in the holy place" (*The Psalms*, Old Testament Library [Philadelphia: Westminster, 1962], p. 488); M. Dahood: "The Lord, who created Sinai as his sanctuary" (*Psalms II, 51–100*, p.143); Cross: "When he came from Sinai with the Holy Ones" (*Canaanite Myth*, p. 102). The issue is hardly settled.

The temple itself is thus regarded as an idol just like the calf in the wilderness through which the Israelites "rejoiced in the work of their hands" (v. 41). The pattern of disobedience leads directly from Mount Sinai to Jerusalem.

Two other New Testament passages develop the Sinai-Zion rivalry hinted at in the Hebrew bible into a symbolic contrast between old and new covenants. First, in Gal. 4:22–26, Paul writes:

> For it is written that Abraham had two sons, one by a slave and one by a free woman. But the son of the slave was born according to the flesh, the son of the free woman through promise. Now this is an allegory: these women are two covenants. One is from Mount Sinai, bearing children for slavery; she is Hagar. Now Hagar is Mount Sinai in Arabia; she corresponds to the present Jerusalem, for she is in slavery with her children. But the Jerusalem above is free, and she is our mother.

What begins as an opposition between Mount Sinai and Mount Zion concludes as a contrast between the earthly and heavenly Jerusalem.[45] Although the allegory is incomplete, its intent seems clear. Paul opposes the old Israel, enslaved under the law given at Sinai, the spiritual descendant of the slave Hagar, represented by the earthly Jerusalem, to the new Israel, the spiritual descendant of the free woman Sarah, represented by the Jerusalem above, "our mother." S. Talmon suggests that the association of Mount Sinai with "primitive nomadism" and of Mount Zion with "cultured, cultivated, civilized life" is behind the allegory. In any case, Zion replaces Sinai and the heavenly replaces the earthly as the locus of God's presence.

A more vivid development of the same symbolic contrast is found in Hebrews. This book, which makes extensive use of wilderness cult imagery—tent, sanctuary, priesthood—to interpret the significance of the Christ event, sets out to prove that the covenant at Sinai is inferior to the covenant through Christ, for Christ "abolishes the first in order to establish the second" (10:9). The climax of the contrast, indeed of the whole book, is the contrast between the goal of the Israelites in the wilderness and the goal of the Christians in this life:[46]

> For you have not come to what may be touched, a blazing fire, and darkness, and gloom, and a tempest, and the sound of a trumpet, and a voice whose words made the hearers entreat that no further messages be spoken to them. For they could not endure the order that was given, "If even a beast touches the mountain, it shall be stoned." Indeed so terrifying was the sight that Moses said, "I tremble with fear." But you have come to Mount Zion and to the city of the living God, the heavenly Jerusalem . . .[12:18–22].

---

[45] I borrow this illustration from Talmon, "Biblical Concept," p. 310.

[46] See J. H. Davies, *A Letter to Hebrews* (London: Cambridge University Press, 1967), p. 46.

Mount Sinai, nameless here, perhaps, to indicate its nullity, is a terrifying sight before which the people shudder and even Moses trembles.[47] Although this physical, earthly place could be "touched," they were commanded not to let even their animals touch it — so fearful was the mountain. Mount Zion, on the other hand, which here shares in the heavenly Jerusalem, is approachable, joyous, and peaceful (vv. 22–24). The angels are arrayed in their celestial best, and perfect men flourish everywhere. So Mount Sinai, obscured in darkness and gloom, represents the old order, while Jerusalem has become "a symbol of the final or ultimate community where God dwells with his own."[48] Again Sinai serves as a symbol of the old, outmoded, rejected.

For the rabbis, however, the Sinai symbol was not eclipsed. Mount Sinai continued to be revered as the site of both theophany and covenant. The midrash praised Sinai for being chosen as the site of the revelation: because of its humility, says one tradition; because idols were not worshipped there, says another. Just as biblical authors retrojected their law codes to Sinai, the rabbis understood their traditions to have been given to Moses on Sinai and thence communicated orally from generation to generation (*m. 'Abot* 1:1). A formula used several times in the Mishnah connects even a *halakah* (ruling) not derivable from the written law to Mount Sinai (e.g., *Peah* 2:6; *Eduy.* 8:7; *Yad.* 4:3).

The Gospel of Matthew depends on this tradition when it has Jesus deliver his new Torah from a mountain. "You have heard it said . . . but I say to you" from a new Mount Sinai. Similarly, the transfiguration scene sets Jesus and his inner circle on "a high mountain apart" (17:1). There Moses and Elijah appear talking to Jesus under "a bright cloud" (v. 5) from which a voice proclaims Jesus as its "beloved son." This scene is calculated to show that the God of Sinai has given Jesus the authority associated with the prophets of Mount Sinai. Thus, for Matthew, Jesus replaces Torah from Sinai.

For Judaism, however, the Sinai symbol remained potent because its meaning was not dependent upon the reverses which history dealt the Jewish people. It was the mountain of the past, the source of Israel's knowledge of God. Because no one knew where it was and no attempt was made to find it, it remained alive in memory only. Mount Sinai, furthermore, played no role in Jewish eschatological expectation. Mount Zion, not Mount Sinai, became the center of the messianic kingdom of God. Mount Sinai, on the contrary, beckoned pilgrims not to itself but to the God and the law which were revealed there.

---

[47] C. Spicq notes that no Pentateuchal tradition has Moses tremble and suggests that the author is dependent upon an aggadic tradition: *L'Épitre aux Hébreux* (Paris: Librairie Lecoffre, 1953), 2:403.

[48] W. D. Davies, *The Gospel and the Land* (Berkeley and Los Angeles: University of California Press, 1974), p. 162, n. 3.

Chapter Five

THE SENSES OF A CENTER

Among the great contributions of the comparative study of religions has been the decoding of basic symbol structures common to many traditions and the revealing of the similar preoccupations of *homo religiosus* expressed through these symbols across religious frontiers. In his articulation of the realm of sacred space in the history of religions, Mircea Eliade discusses a variety of images that express the "symbolism of the center." The pillar, ladder, tree, vine, and mountain can each symbolize the communication link between heaven, earth, and underworld at the spot where the sacred has manifested itself. This spot "constitutes a break in the homogeneity of space," a place around which the world is ordered.[1] It is considered, variously, the highest place on earth, the navel or midpoint of the world, the place from which creation began. Eliade constructs an "archetype" consisting of all the meanings a particular image carries in world religions. The task of the historian of religions is to study particular cultures in light of that archetype, to "elucidate the reasons why such a culture has retained, developed, or forgotten a symbolic aspect of [for example] the Cosmic Tree. In so doing, he will be led to penetrate more deeply into the soul of this culture, and will learn to differentiate it from others."[2]

Behind this analysis seems to be the assumption of a *homo symbolicus* who generates local manifestations of universal symbols. Although the results of such an analysis can be provocative, the method risks unhinging the symbolic from the concrete. The method works "from the top down," on a level of abstraction which can forsake the concrete, historical culture which produces the symbol for the sake of comparative parallels.

In a suggestive piece that explores the various senses in which Jerusalem is a "center" for Judaism, J. Z. Smith claims "the historian of religion's privilege of disregarding chronological and geographical considerations; of comparing and bringing together, as revealing, texts from

[1] Mircea Eliade, *The Sacred and the Profane* (New York: Harper and Row, 1959), p. 37.

[2] Mircea Eliade, "Methodological Remarks on the Study of Religious Symbolism," *The History of Religions: Essays in Methodology*, ed. M. Eliade and J. Kitagawa (Chicago and London: University of Chicago Press, 1959), p. 95.

widely different periods and contexts of Jewish history."[3] While, as he so interestingly demonstrates, comparative data can sensitize the analyst to nuances he might otherwise have missed, ignoring historical and geographical considerations risks taking data out of context and missing internal development.

In this paper we discuss Jerusalem as a center "from the bottom up." We consider the concrete historical setting in which the center symbolism takes root and the manner in which cultural transformation affects the perception of the center from biblical through Roman times. If, as Clifford Geertz says, a symbol "gives form to experience and points to action," as experience changes, so should its symbolic representation.[4] In brief, we first discuss the absence of a single center in earliest Israel as a backdrop for the emergence of the Jerusalem center. We can then see with new clarity how Zion, the sacred mountain, rises out of monarchial experience. Third, we note that exile and diaspora provoke a shift in the conception of the center, crystallizing in the omphalos-metropolis symbol of Hellenistic Jewish literature. Finally, we observe the ambivalent attitude toward the Jerusalem center in regnant Judaism following the second fall of the city over against parallel developments among Samaritans and Christians. This comparison leads to some concluding thoughts about the holiness of place in Judaism.

Centerlessness

The prominent role of Jerusalem, in biblical times as political and cultic center of Judah and in post-biblical times as a focus of Jewish territorial and spiritual aspirations, makes it easy to forget that this sacred center was not always sacred or a center for Israel. A Jebusite fortress belonging to none of the tribes, Jerusalem in pre-monarchial days was a foreign enclave in the midst of the Israelite land of settlement. To appreciate the transformation which rendered this site God's "holy mountain, beautiful in elevation, the joy of all the earth" (Ps. 48:3), we must consider the geographical focus of those early days.

Not one but a multiplicity of centers characterized the settlement period.[5] Each clan or tribe or group of tribes had its shrine. Dan in the north, Shechem, Gibeon, Gilgal, Bethel in the center of the country, and Hebron and Beersheba in the south, for instance, could claim theophanies or various sacred objects which attracted the allegiance of the surrounding inhabitants. Although many such sites were undoubtedly inherited from Israel's Canaanite predecessors, legend baptised them in the name of Yahweh, and he was invoked and worshipped in them.

---

[3] Jonathan Z. Smith, "Earth and Gods," *The Journal of Religion* 49 (1969): 107.

[4] Clifford Geertz, *Islam Observed*, p. 95.

[5] See S. Talmon, *"har, gibh'āh,"* pp. 443–44.

Several mountain peaks, in fact, likely were revered as holy places prior to Mount Zion. The loftiest peak in the land, snowcapped Mount Hermon (possibly derived from *herem*, "consecrated, sacred") was probably sacred to the Canaanites. On Mount Carmel Elijah rebuilt an altar to Yahweh (1 Kings 18:30). Another was built on Mount Ebal (Josh. 8:30), while the valley between Mount Ebal and Mount Gerizim was the scene of a ceremony of blessings and curses (Josh. 8:33ff.). From Mount Tabor, which joined the territories of Issachar, Zebulun, and Naphtali, a war of Yahweh against the Canaanites was launched. Mount Sinai, treated with legendary awe in the Bible, may have been a pilgrimage site for southern tribes. Several known shrines, such as Bethel and Gibeon, were also located on hilltops. This is only a natural development considering the mountainous character of the land and the sense of authority that a mountain peak commands.

Clearly, none of these "centers" was the political or cultic locus of order which Jerusalem eventually became. In fact, if we seek a single focus of attention for Israel's first two centuries in the land, we must look not to a center but to the periphery. According to the books of Joshua and Judges, the principal activities of the Israelites during the pre-monarchial period were staking out territory and defending the frontiers against enemy incursions. In this enterprise, Israel's mountains provided a measure of real security because Canaanite chariotry could not maneuver there, yet the Philistine threat from the coastal plain remained constant until David's time (2 Sam. 5:22ff.). The ancient ark of the covenant often accompanied the fighters in these border battles. Conceived to be the throne of Yahweh, this holy object rested in various of the amphictyonic centers, investing them with the presence of Yahweh. In essence a portable shrine, the ark, when brought to the front, was thought to assure victory. Its mobility suited well a people whose preoccupation seems to have been the establishment of secure and recognized borders. God was on the perimeter, fighting for Israel. When the ark was captured, "The glory departs from Israel" (1 Sam. 4: 21). Later, when it returned, it was kept at Kiryat Yearim, not far from the Philistine border. There it could act as a shield against the enemy. Later still, Saul, in his pursuit of David, was drawn continually to the southern border of the land where David and his commandos raided the enemies of Judah. Real power lay not in Saul's capital of Gibeah, but in the hands of David. The source of order stayed mainly on the border. Thus, the pre-monarchial period lacked a single, unifying geographical center.

The Sacred Mountain

Stepping into the power vacuum left by the demise of the raving Saul, David seized upon the plan which was to end the "center vacuum" as well. Seven years after being proclaimed king in Hebron, he captured Jerusalem in an apparent bloodless coup and made it his personal possession, the "city of David" (2 Sam. 5:7). It soon became the capital of an expanding empire, new home for the ancient ark (2 Sam. 6:16), and, under Solomon, the site of the "house of Yahweh." In one master stroke, David eliminated a foreign hamlet, elevated his capital above tribal rivalries, and harnessed the power of the revered tribal sanctum to sanctify the new city.

Indeed, the demographic and geographic transformation of Israel which David wrought demanded a center as the old tribal structure had not. By subduing the Philistines, subjecting surrounding peoples, and eliminating Canaanite power pockets, David homogenized the Israelite territory. At the same time, the ethnic composition of Israel broadened as vassal groups began to assimilate. Furthermore, mercenary soldiers, foreign advisors, and royal princesses and their parties altered the human face of the capital. From a tribal confederacy on the defense, Israel had become an imperialist power on the offense. With the borders secured, attention shifted to the center. The theo-political need now was to unify a multicultural population extending over a vast and varied geographical area. The royal ideology, with its emphasis on king, temple, and city, developed to provide a rallying point for the empire.[6]

Thus, although Jerusalem was an undistinguished fortress town with no roots in Israelite history, it nonetheless became the geographic hub of the monarchy. When the psalmists and prophets sought to express the senses in which Jerusalem was a center for Israel, however, they did not speak of the strategic considerations which led David to select the city. The political and military factors of interest to critical historians did not exercise the "sacred historians" who composed the Zion tradition. For them, these factors, if they were differentiated at all, were subordinated to the celebration of the divine favor believed to be manifest in the city's success. They spoke in symbolic language of the meaning the city had come to have. Foremost among the symbols they employed is the mountain. Of the various epithets for the city found in the Bible—City of Judah, Holy City, City of the Temple, etc.—none is more prominent than "Mount Zion" and "the holy mountain." Each term, in fact, appears thirteen times in Psalms and in Isaiah, the prophet most closely linked to the royal ideology, and rather miscellaneously through the other prophetic books.[7] The number and distribution of the epithets

---

[6] This line of argument is indebted to S. Talmon, "The Biblical Concept of Jerusalem," pp. 300–316, and "Jerusalem in Ancient Times," *CCAR Journal* 24 (1977): 11–18. See also the discussion of J. J. M. Roberts, "The Davidic Origin," pp. 340–43.

[7] The distribution of the terms outside of Isaiah and Psalms is as follows: Mount Zion (*har ṣiyyôn*): Joel 3:5, 4:17; Mic. 4:7; Obad. 17,21; Lam. 5:18. The Holy Mountain (*har haqqodeš*): Jer. 31:23; Ezek. 20:40; 28:14; Joel 2:1; 4:17; Obad. 16; Zeph. 3:11; Zech. 8:3; Dan. 9:16, 20; 11:45.

indicates the popularity of the symbol, and the richness of the imagery with which it is pictured suggests, as we shall see, its hold on the biblical imagination.

But why should Jerusalem as a center have been conceived as a mountain? First, the geophysical setting of the city provided a basis for the designation. The temple area is a small hill with steep sides, while the Ophel to the south, the original fortress that David captured, was thought impenetrable because of its hilltop site (2 Sam. 5:6). Yet the temple hill is flanked by the higher Mount of Olives to the east, so geography does not fully explain the phenomenon.

Second, biblical scholars point out the prominent role of sacred mountains as homes of the gods in the ancient Near East, especially in Canaan. Richard Clifford has demonstrated that literary traditions of the Canaanite sacred mountains of the gods El and Baal became attached to Zion.[8] Ronald Clements has shown that in Canaanite myth the story of Baal's reign on Mount Zaphon symbolically established the hegemony of Baal over the land in which his devotees lived. Similarly, Yahweh's reign on Mount Zion was likely a way of expressing his dominance over the land that formerly was Baal's.[9] The biblical poets, by employing the mountain symbol, spoke in the common language of the ancient Near East to announce the new status of their capital, Jerusalem.

Third, the Israelites may simply have inherited sacred mountain traditions about Zion from their Jebusite predecessors in the city. It is very likely that the threshing floor which David purchased from Araunah for an altar to Yahweh (2 Sam. 24:18–25) was already a holy place, for threshing floors were often cultic sites. And the Chronicler identifies this threshing floor as the site on which the temple is to be erected (1 Chron. 22:1). Furthermore, many scholars hold that, after his bloodless coup in Jerusalem, David took the priests already there into his own retinue. With them came their myths about the sacred mountain Zion. In opposition to this theory, J. J. M. Roberts has argued that the Zion tradition cannot be derived from the Jebusite cult and that its source lies rather in the Davidic-Solomonic era.[10] Whatever the sources of the tradition, however, it functioned because it expressed the new theo-political reality of the imperial capital.

Finally, for the mountain symbol to seize the biblical imagination, it also needed to encapsulate Israelite experience. A fourth reason, then,

[8] Clifford, *The Cosmic Mountain*, pp. 131–60.

[9] R. E. Clements, *God and Temple* (Philadelphia: Fortress, 1965), pp. 9, 50–53.

[10] Roberts, "The Davidic Origin," pp. 329–44. The most extreme statement of Davidic dependence upon Jebusites is that of George Mendenhall, "The Monarchy," *Interpretation* 29 (1975): 163: "though it cannot be proven, there seems to me little doubt that most of the bureaucratic substructure under King David was inherited from the previous Jebusite regime."

that the center became a sacred mountain was Israel's favorable evaluation of the real mountains. Israel settled in the hill country of Canaan
which remained its base of operations even at the height of the Davidic
empire. Its enemies, in fact, recognized Israel as a hill people worship-
ping mountain gods (1 Kings 20:23). The Deuteronomist, reflecting the
positive Israelite attitude toward its hilly land, characterizes Canaan as
"a land of hills and valleys, which drinks water by the rain of heaven, a
land which the Lord your God cares for . . ." (Deut. 11:11f.). In biblical
poetry, similarly, mountains serve as figures of permanence, security,
fertility. Significantly, Mount Zion-Jerusalem was drawn with these
same images; the sacred mountain, as we have seen (chapter three),
absorbed those qualities perceived as praiseworthy in the mountains in
general.

Having examined why the mountain emerged as the most characteristic symbol for the center during the monarchy, we can identify the
senses of center which the symbol represents. The imagery with which
Mount Zion is described reflects three basic centering functions: military, cultic, and irenic. The military imagery, first of all, presents
Yahweh as a divine warrior battling kings and peoples from his base on
Mount Zion.[11] This *Völkerskampf*, which appears very widely in prophets
(e.g., Isa. 29:6–8; 31:4; Joel 4; Mic. 4:11–13; Zech. 12:14) and Psalms
(e.g., Pss. 2; 46; 48) is sometimes past and sometimes future. Mount
Zion itself is pictured as a fortress besieged but ultimately secure
(Ps. 46f.). God is Israel's "sure defense" within the mountain fortress
(Ps. 48:4).

> Walk about Zion, go round about her,
>   number her towers,
> consider well her ramparts,
>   go through her citadels;
> that you may tell the next generation
>   that this is God,
>   our God for ever and ever.
> He will be our guide forever [Ps. 48:13–15].

The topographic setting of Jerusalem even lends support to this portrait.
"The mountains are round about Jerusalem, and the Lord is round
about his people from this time forth and forever more" (Ps. 125:2).
The battle imagery may well reflect actual revolts of the kings of the
vassal states in the Davidic empire.[12] At least it reveals a preoccupation
with the security of the city often put to the test during the monarchy.
Until Babylon, "the destroying mountain" (Jer. 51:25), captured the
city, however, it remained the center of military and, hence, political
power for Judah. The mountain fortress image epitomizes that power.

---

[11] See Clifford, *The Cosmic Mountain*, pp. 143–50.
[12] Roberts, "The Davidic Origin," 343–44.

Because the temple was built there, Jerusalem became, second, the cultic center, eventually displacing officially all other shrines. The temple was understood to be the earthly "house of Yahweh," though the more sensitive Deuteronomist and priestly writers have only his "name" or "glory" dwell there. Yahweh himself "chose" Zion for his dwelling place (Pss. 78; 132); according to Isaiah (14:32) he "founded" it as he founded the earth or the universe.[13] On his "holy mountain," God hears human prayers (Ps. 3:5), "adopts" and anoints his king (Ps. 2:6), judges in righteousness (Ps. 99:9). On the mountain in the temple the boundary between heaven and earth is erased. Isaiah there sees Yahweh's heavenly throne (6:1); the holy mountain is Yahweh's "footstool" (Ps. 99:5,9). On the mountain, its top piercing the clouds, the communication channel to God is open to the initiated (Ps. 24:3f.). Although the cultic centering function of Jerusalem was operative from David's time, with the collapse of the state it becomes more prominent in the literature. Then the military imagery of Zion ceased to reflect the real situation while the cultic "holy mountain" remained potent even for exiled Jews.

Similarly, the irenic centering function of the sacred mountain increased in importance in the later period. Although peace and righteousness were always associated with the ideal of Jerusalem, the monarchial city rarely enjoyed either.[14] Nonetheless, Mount Zion is seen as a source of blessing and peace to land and people as long as Yahweh dwells there.

> Praise the Lord, O Jerusalem!
> Praise your God, O Zion.
> For he strengthens the bars of your gates;
>   he blesses your sons within you.
> He makes peace in your borders;
>   he fills you with the finest of the wheat [Ps. 147:12–14].

The mountains of Zion attract the dew of Hermon, and from Zion fertility radiates to the land (Ps. 133:3). But if Yahweh should leave Zion, the chaotic wilderness would encroach (Jer. 12:7–10). When the temple actually is destroyed, "Mount Zion lies desolate, jackals prowl over it" (Lam. 5:19).

But the richest irenic imagery occurs in several futuristic oracles where the mountain is the hub of a land and people at peace. Isaiah envisions a time when the temple mount "shall be established at the head of the mountains, and exalted from among the hills" (2:2).

---

[13] Roland de Vaux, "Jerusalem and the Prophets," *Interpreting the Prophetic Tradition*, ed. H. M. Orlinsky (Cincinnati: Hebrew Union College Press, 1969), p. 286.

[14] Norman Porteous, "Jerusalem-Zion: The Growth of a Symbol," *Verbannung und Heimkehr*, Beiträge zur Geschichte und Theologie Israels im 6. und 5.-Jahrhundert v. Chr., ed. A. Kuschke (Tübingen: J. C. B. Mohr, 1961), esp. pp. 239–40.

Reversing a proverb which called men to war (Joel 4:10), he sees that people "will beat their swords into plowshares and their spears into pruning hooks." Not war but Torah comes forth from Zion (2:3). Ezekiel's new Jerusalem, the entire city, is set on a "very high mountain" (40:2). A river gushes from below the temple, flows to the Dead Sea, and turns the wilderness into a fertile garden like Eden (47:1–12). In Zechariah's picture, the land will be turned into a plain, but "Jerusalem shall remain aloft" (14:10) with rivers flowing both eastward and westward. Third Isaiah sees the new Jerusalem to be bigger and more splendid by far than its predecessor. Its "gates shall be open continually" (60:11), and the temple "shall be called a house of prayer for all peoples" (56:7). The peace which the present does not know is projected in these oracles into the future. It emanates from a new Jerusalem pictured as a higher, more magnificent holy mountain towering above a regenerated land of Israel. Like a magnet it attracts the nations and scattered Israel.

Biblical literature thus reflects three centering functions of Jerusalem expressed through the symbol of the mountain. They derived from the actual experience of Israel at war, at prayer, and in hope of peace. The symbol grew out of Israelite life and reflection and acquired new meanings as that life developed.

Metropolis and Omphalos

The glorious visions of the prophets did not materialize, and post-exilic Zion was but a shadow of its former self. Remembering the glory of the first temple the old folks weep at the commencement of the building of the second (Ezra 3:12). The reported ambidexterity of Nehemiah's builders of the city wall, with weapons in one hand and building materials in the other (Neh. 4:17), underscores the fragile hold of the returnees on their city. Those exiles who could not sing the Lord's song in a foreign land found it difficult to do so even in their own for a time. Now a buffer zone against Egypt in the vast Persian empire, the land of Israel was itself diaspora, occupied by foreigners, and the law of Moses was imposed by the authority of Artaxerxes, the Persian emperor.

Although the literary sources for the Persian period are thin, it is possible to discern the beginning of a new sense of center that achieved symbolic clarity only later in the Hellenistic period. With the exile comes a rise in the "horizontal" imagery of geophysical center. On the eve of the first "return to Zion," Second Isaiah envisions the ransom of scattered Israel from the four cardinal directions and from "the ends of the earth" (Isa. 43:5f.), suggesting that Jerusalem lies in the middle of the exiles. Third Isaiah continues this theme, speaking not only of the return of Israel from afar but also of the coming of the kings, the nations, and their wealth to Jerusalem. During this era, moreover, pilgrimage rituals were definitively formulated. Their attraction to Jews in both Judea and diaspora throughout the second temple period is another indication of the perception of Jerusalem as geographic center. Moreover, even prayer said when facing Jerusalem was believed to be efficacious for those in exile (Dan. 6:10; cf. 1 Kings 8:44,48); the horizontal connection to the holy temple transcended distance.

By the latter part of the second temple period, the Jewish diaspora had grown greatly in size, extent, and influence. Emigration from Judea, conversion, and a high birth rate contributed to a diaspora community estimated to be three times as large as the Palestinian population. Approximately one in ten Roman citizens was a Jew, and in the important city of Alexandria nearly two-fifths of the inhabitants may have been Jewish.[15] For most of these Jews, physical connections with the "homeland" must have been tenuous, yet Jerusalem was still a center. In the first century, Philo crystallizes this Hellenistic sense of center in *The Embassy to Gaius* when Agrippa proclaims:

> I as you know am by birth a Jew and my native city is Jerusalem in which is situated the sacred shrine of the most high God. . . . While she, as I have said, is my native city, she is also the mother city (*metropolis*) not of one country Judaea but of most of the others in virtue of the colonies sent out at divers times to the neighboring lands. . . not only are the mainlands full of Jewish colonies but also the most highly esteemed of the islands . . . [36:278–283].

Philo is sensitive to the potential chaos of diasporic existence. If the temple is the earthly dwelling place of Yahweh from which blessing flows to land and people, how can the holy be sustained outside the land? By employing and expanding the Greek idea of *metropolis*, he makes Jerusalem not the political capital of Judea but the spiritual capital of the Roman *ecumene*. Whatever his place of birth, every Jew is born spiritually in Jerusalem, his source and foundation.[16] Diaspora is not, for Philo, a punishment for sin, but rather a demographic necessity.

> For so populous are the Jews that no one country can hold them, and therefore they settle in very many of the most prosperous countries in Europe and Asia both in the islands and on the mainland, and while they hold the Holy City where stands the sacred Temple of the most high God to be their mother city, yet those which are theirs by inheritance from their fathers, grandfathers, and ancestors even farther back, are in each

---

[15] Salo Baron, *A Social and Religious History of the Jews* (New York: Columbia University Press, 1952), 1:171.

[16] See J. .A. Seeligman, "Jerusalem in Jewish-Hellenistic Thought," *Judah and Jerusalem*, The Twelfth Archaeological Convention (Jerusalem: Israel Exploration Society, 1957), pp. 196–98 (in Hebrew).

case accounted by them to be their fatherland in which they were born and reared. [*Flaccus* 7:45–6].

Here Philo establishes the principle of "dual loyalty." Diaspora Jews are fully Jews by virtue of their recognition of Jerusalem as their holy mother city, but they also demand to be recognized as citizens in the lands where they live and not merely guests in host countries.

Alexandria, Philo's "fatherland," was a center not only of the Jewish diaspora but of the Greek diaspora as well. This was the richest point of confluence of the two cultures, perhaps because both Jews and Greeks were foreigners asserting their superiority over the natives and each other. Philo argues that Judaism, despite its lack of political power, is coterminous with the empire and is, in fact, its spiritual heart. The following description of the Greek diaspora could equally well have been written of the Jewish diaspora.

> Their unity was not political, as it never had been in the long history of the Greeks, nor was it racial. It was . . . a unity of civilization, the bond between members of this unit being identity of language, of education, of mentality, of group organization, of mode of life, and of religious conceptions. This bond united settlers living in small and scattered groups, surrounded by multitudes of men of a quite different type and some of them highly civilized.[17]

But, above all, the Jews had Jerusalem, now conceived not as a mountain but primarily as a metropolis. As the mountain was the symbol of empire in the first temple period, the metropolis was the symbol of *ecumene* in the second temple period.

Hellenistic Jerusalem, moreover, was considered not only a metropolis; it was also an omphalos, the navel of the earth, the nurturing source of Jewry. The omphalos symbol was well established in Greek culture. From at least classical times the shrine of Apollo at Delphi was considered by the Greeks to be the earth's navel, the source of nourishment and truth. As Socrates puts it:

> To Apollo the god of Delphi, there remains the ordering of the greatest and noblest and chiefest things of all. . . .The institution of temples and sacrifices, and the entire service of gods, demigods, and heroes; also the ordering of repositories of the dead, and the rites which have to be observed by him who would propitiate the inhabitants of the world below. These are matters of which we are ignorant ourselves, and as founders of a city we should be unwise in trusting them to any interpreter but our ancestral deity. He is the god who sits in the centre, on the navel of the earth, and he is the interpreter of religion to all mankind [Plato, *The Republic* 427b, c].

[17] J. Rostovtzeff, *The Social and Economic History of the Hellenistic World*, (Oxford: Oxford University Press, 1941), 2:1057.

Even earlier, Delphi was associated with Ge, the earth goddess. According to legend, Zeus determined the location of the omphalos by releasing two eagles, one from each end of the earth, which met at Delphi. The egg-shaped stone which once rested in the inner sanctuary of the temple was decorated with two birds, one on either side, representing the two eagles. This sacred stone was associated with the worship of the earth goddess. Many of the Greek cities in the diaspora traced their foundations to instructions from the oracle at Delphi. It is this Greek omphalos conception which Hellenistic Jewish writers adopted to describe their mother city. Only in the Hellenistic period did the omphalos symbolism become explicit because only then did it "center" a diaspora Jewry that found in it the means to express order amid the potential chaos of diaspora. (Several scholars, on the basis of some biblical passages and allusions, have claimed that the conception of Jerusalem as omphalos played an important role in the worship of the first temple. On the contrary, as an *explicit* symbol, the omphalos emerges clearly only in the Hellenistic period.)[18]

Philo, in his appeal to Gaius, for instance, tells of a journey of Gaius' grandfather, Marcus Agrippa, "from the coast to the capital situated in the center of the land" (37:294). Similarly, in his description of the land of Judea, Josephus says that Jerusalem is in the very center between Jaffa and the river Jordan "for which reason the town has sometimes, not inaptly, been called the 'navel' of the country" (*War* 3:5,52). Josephus, who, as a military commander, certainly knew the lay of the land, nevertheless includes this characterization of Jerusalem. Earlier, the Letter of Aristeas had located Jerusalem "in the middle of the whole of Judea on top of a mountain of considerable altitude" (v. 83). The "centering" of Jerusalem extended to the location of the temple itself, for Josephus quotes Hecataeus who places the temple at the center of the city (*Against Apion* 22, 197). Probably neither the

---

[18] The arguments are of two kinds. The first purports to find explicit testimony that Jerusalem was regarded as the navel of the earth (e.g., Ezek. 5:5; Ps. 74:12). See, for instance, Bernhard Anderson, *Creation versus Chaos: The Reinterpretation of Mythical Symbolism in the Bible* (New York: Association Press, 1967), p 117; Brevard Childs, *Myth and Reality in the Old Testament* (London: SCM Press, 1962), pp. 86–88. On closer inspection, however, the phrase translated in each case as "in the center, midst, of the earth" has been so rendered without taking into account the many other appearances of the phrase lacking this special meaning. Similarly the phrase *ṭabbûr hā'āreṣ*, which appears only twice in the Bible (Judg. 9:37; Ezek 38:12), is first translated as *omphalos* in the Septuagint. In fact, the literary contexts do not support this translation (Seeligman, "Jerusalem," p. 204). The second argument claims that the omphalos myth, known from Delphi and elsewhere, is the "determining factor which links together a number of . . . cultic practices and beliefs of the temple worship in Jerusalem." See Samuel Terrien, "The Omphalos Myth and Hebrew Religion," *Vetus Testamentum* 20 (1970): 317. These are snake-worship, chthonian rites, the solar cult, male prostitution, and bisexuality. This is highly speculative. See Talmon's discussion of the issue in "*har; gibh'āh*," pp. 437–38.

author of the letter nor Hecataeus had been to Jerusalem, but both picture it according to the regnant Hellenistic conception.

Despite the emphasis on Jerusalem as omphalos, however, the old sacred mountain symbolism was not dropped. Not only Aristeas but also Jubilees retains it. "And [Noah] knew that the Garden of Eden is the holy of holies, and the dwelling of the Lord, and Mount Sinai the center of the desert and Mount Zion the center of the navel of the earth: these three were created as holy places facing each other" (8:19). Here the Bible's two sacred mountains, *par excellence*, become geographical mid-points, designations not accorded them in the biblical text. While for Josephus, Philo, and Aristeas, Jerusalem was the center of Judea only, for Jubilees, it is the "center of the navel of the earth." Here two originally distinct motifs, Zion as highest mountain and Jerusalem as omphalos, are combined.[19] But mountain symbolism was on the wane. The isolation of diaspora Jews from the real mountains of the land of Israel is reflected in a caricature of their actual dimensions. In Judith, for example, the mountains of Israel have become the chief means of the people's defense. Their enemies say, "For these people, the Israelites, do not rely on their spears but on the height of the mountains where they live, for it is not easy to reach the tops of their mountains" (7:10). While Israel's mountains did afford it protection, here that role is exaggerated in folk-tale style. Similarly, Judith prays against Assyrian designs "against thy consecrated house, and against the top of Zion" (9:13).

The symbol of Jerusalem as metropolis and omphalos thus anchored the far-flung Jewish community by providing it a physical and a spiritual center. Under the influence of Greek thought, the Hellenistic Jewish writers developed a symbol which, like the earlier mountain fortress, expressed the new theo-political reality. The center, not of everyday life, but of the great heritage of the Jews, Jerusalem was the mother city to which one was connected ethnically and spiritually. Jerusalem was the distant city toward which Jews looked nostalgically. Synagogues faced Jerusalem and pilgrims journeyed there. Jerusalem became the "center out there."[20] National pride caused Jews to regard the city as their omphalos, the physical source and center of spiritual truth in the Roman ecumene.

The Ambiguous Center

If the mythologians of the first temple focused on Zion the sacred mountain, and Hellenistic thinkers understood Jerusalem as the omphalos of Judea and metropolis of Jewry, what was to happen when the

---

[19] Seeligman, "Jerusalem in Jewish Hellenistic Thought," p. 203.
[20] The phrase is Victor Turner's in "The Center Out There: Pilgrim's Goal," pp. 191–230.

temple and city were again destroyed? If the exiles in Babylon could remember their beloved Mount Zion and take courage in Ezekiel's visions of a high mountain and a new temple, could the Jews in the Roman diaspora put their hopes in the renewal of a metropolis they had never seen? Could Mount Zion-Jerusalem perdure as a centering symbol or was the diaspora to be geographically centerless? Whereas the diaspora was created by the destruction of the first temple, it was an ongoing entity at the time of the second. Did this mean that Jerusalem was expendable?

Yes and no. On the the one hand, the loss of the temple and the city was mourned bitterly. The ritual grieving for the loss of the temple on the ninth of Av and the later creation of the midrash on Lamentations (*Lamentations Rabbah*) testify to a deep meditation on the reasons for and consequences of the fall of the temple. Apocalyptists addressed the sense of loss with visions of the heavenly Jerusalem descending to earth. "And Zion will come and be made manifest to all people, prepared and built, as you saw the mountain carved out without hands" (2 Esd. 13:36). Less extravagantly, the Passover Seder included a prayer for the rebuilding of the city (*m. Pesahim* 10:6). The opinion that the temple service was one of three things sustaining the world (*m. 'Abot* 1:2) was treasured even when this service had ended. In fact, concern with the now defunct sacrifical system (*m. Kodashim*) witnesses not only to a hope for the restoration of the temple but to a preoccupation with this past center. The omphalos had become temporal; it was buried in the past or projected into the future, but the exile of the present had no definite center.

On the other hand, life went on without Jerusalem. In many ways, in fact, Torah performed a centering function for Judaism in the absence of temple and city. It mediated the divine presence: "If two sit together and words of the Torah are spoken between them, the Shekhinah rests between them" (*m. 'Abot* 3:2). It guided one to deeds of personal sacrifice which now replaced the animal sacrifice of the temple.[21] The "sure defense" of Judaism, once symbolized by the city walls, became now the "fence around the Torah." The synagogue came fully into its own as a place of prayer and study of Torah. The omphalos, theoretically still in Jerusalem, practically was shattered into as many pieces as there were Jewish communities.

So the Jewish attitude toward Jerusalem was ambivalent. Attachment to the city coexisted with a mode of life for which Jerusalem was not essential. Judaism did not become totally diasporic. Zion remained the holy city, yet in rabbinic *aggadot* geographical imagery gave way to fanciful descriptions reminiscent of those of Ezekiel and Zechariah. One

---

[21] See Jacob Neusner's good discussion in *First Century Judaism in Crisis* (Nashville and New York: Abingdon, 1975), pp. 168–70.

dictum claims, "The temple is higher than all the land of Israel and the land of Israel is higher than all the lands" (*b. Kiddushin* 59a). In the Mishnah the earth is pictured in concentric circles of holiness emanating from the Holy of Holies: "There are ten degrees of holiness. The Land of Israel is holier than any other land. The walled cities of the Land of Israel are still more holy . . . . Within the wall of Jerusalem is still more holy. . . ." (*m. Kelim* 1:6–9). The much later *Tanḥuma* sees Zion as the omphalos in quite a literal sense. According to it the construction of the earth was begun at its central point, the foundation stone of the temple, the *'eben šĕtiyāh*, and spread outward.[22] Rashi, however, conceived the world to have been created from its sides inward with the *'eben šĕtiyāh* as the capstone. One can justly wonder how seriously the rabbis themselves took these playful cosmogonies. Alongside exaggerated but understandable descriptions of Jerusalem as the midpoint of Judea and mother city of the diaspora in the Letter of Aristeas, Josephus, and Philo are the aggadic stories of the rabbis which transformed it into the center of the cosmos.

Regnant Judaism's ambivalent sense of center with respect to Jerusalem comes into sharper focus when it is compared with the senses of center in two closely related religions. Samaritanism and Christianity, both crystallizing concurrently with rabbinic Judaism, displayed quite different symbolisms of the center. These can be correlated with the differing experiences of the two groups. They illustrate the range of possibilities of center symbolism available to "Judaism" in the broadest sense.

The Samaritans, relying on Pentateuchal traditions, claimed the ancient holiness of Mount Gerizim from early second temple days. On this their sacred mountain, they built a temple during the early Hellenistic period rivaling that in Jerusalem. Mount Gerizim, not Mount Zion, was the mountain God had chosen, according to their tenth commandment. The fourth century C. E. *Memar Marqah* devotes one of its chapters to glorifying Mount Gerizim, accounted as one of the seven best things in the world.[23] Here the sacred mountain becomes the center of time, attracting the major events of Samaritan sacred history. Here Adam was created from its dust; here Noah sacrificed, Abraham bound Isaac, Jacob dreamed, Joseph and Joshua were buried. Toward Mount Gerizim Moses turned as he lay down atop Mount Nebo to die. The mountain is given thirteen names in the Torah, including "the mountain of the East" (Gen. 10:30), Bethel (Gen. 12:8), and "the Lord will provide"

---

[22] Louis Ginzberg, *The Legends of the Jews* (Philadelphia: Jewish Publication Society, 1913), 1:12.

[23] *Memar Marqah: The Teaching of Marqah*, vol 2, ed. and trans. John Macdonald, Beihefte zur Zeitschrift für die Alttestamentliche Wissenschaft, 84 (Berlin: Verlag Alfred Topelmann, 1963), p. 73.

(Gen. 22:14). To this day, the annual Passover sacrifice occurs on the holy mountain, and the Samaritans living elsewhere make pilgrimage for its celebration.

That the sacred mountain remained the centering symbol for the Samaritans as it did not for the Jews is due, at least in part, to demography. Although at periods in its history, the Samaritan diaspora was sizable, it never was as significant for the faith as the Jewish diaspora was for Judaism. Creative renewal emanated from Samaria, and diaspora communities were, relatively speaking, transitory. Furthermore, although their temple was destroyed by the Hasmoneans, the Samaritans retained control of their mountain throughout history. They were never separated from the "one true sanctuary." Furthermore, unlike Jerusalem, the mountain was purely a cultic site. The Samaritan capital lay elsewhere, at Sebastia, until it was destroyed. So the real mountain Gerizim remained the locus of Samaritan religious life. For Judaism the diaspora experience, first in Babylon and then in the Hellenistic world, gave rise to the ambiguous sense of center. But Samaritanism, a fundamentally non-diasporic faith, did not transcend its geographic starting point.

Early Christianity, on the other hand, soon became thoroughly diasporic. The national and geographic ties that the early Christians had with their Jewish co-religionists were completely shattered by the fall of the second temple, which the Christians took as vindication of their own cause. Although attitudes toward the "holy land" differed among the early Christian writers, the increasingly Gentile composition of the predominantly diasporic "church" was bound to loosen attachment to a place few had ever known.

It is true that Jerusalem is important in the New Testament. Luke, for example, gives Jerusalem especial prominence. The birth story of John, Jesus' childhood visit to the temple, his determination to deliver his message there, and his post-resurrection appearances nearby all show Luke's desire to depict Christianity as proceeding from the geographical and spiritual heart of Judaism. Yet even before the fall of the real Jerusalem, its hold on the Christian mind was eclipsed by that of the heavenly Jerusalem. Paul, as we saw above, reads the Hagar-Sarah rivalry as an "allegory" corresponding to the contrast between the enslaved earthly Jerusalem of the Jews and the heavenly Jerusalem of those in Christ (Gal. 4:21–31). "But the Jerusalem above is free, and she is our *mother*" (v. 26). Not the earthly but the heavenly Jerusalem is the metropolis of the Christian community.[24] The author of Hebrews later makes a similar contrast (12:18–24). He declares that "the city which has foundations, whose builder and maker is God" (11:10), to which even Abraham looked forward, is this heavenly Jerusalem. Like

---

[24] Talmon makes this point in "The Biblical Concept of Jerusalem," p. 310.

Christians awaiting the manifestation of that prepared city, the patriarchs "were strangers and exiles on the earth" (11:13). "For here we have no lasting city, but we seek the city which is to come" (13:14). The Christian diaspora had no earthly omphalos.[25]

Moreover, in the Fourth Gospel, when the Samaritan woman asks Jesus the location of the proper worship site, he replies, "Woman, believe me, the hour is coming when neither on this mountain [Gerizim] nor in Jerusalem will you worship the Father. . . . God is spirit, and those who worship him must worship in spirit and truth" (4:21,24). Both the sacred mountain of the Samaritans and the holy city of the Jews are repudiated. Holiness is not connected to a place; Christianity has become divorced from the Jewish attachment to Jerusalem. Space forbids discussion of the manner in which Christ became the new centering symbol, absorbing the functions of city and temple. W. D. Davies summarizes this point well: "The New Testament finds holy space wherever Christ is or has been; it personalizes 'holy space' in Christ, who, as a figure in History, is rooted in the land; he cleansed the Temple and died in Jerusalem, and lends his glory to these and to the places where he was, but as Living Lord, he is also free to move wherever he wills."[26] The early Christian sense of center, then, was not focused on Jerusalem. As the fully diasporic religion, Christianity contrasted sharply with locative Samaritanism and did not share Judaism's ambivalent relationship to the Jerusalem center.

Conclusion

Although we have confirmed comparativists' conclusions that Jerusalem as a sacred center was symbolized as a sacred mountain and a metropolis-omphalos, we have seen that it was perceived in those ways at different times for quite pragmatic reasons. During the monarchy, the royal apologists painted Jerusalem in the colors of the culture of Syria-Canaan, as a sacred mountain. During the second temple era, Hellenistic Jewish writers conceived Jerusalem as a Greek style metropolis and omphalos. In the first case, Israel's real experience with the mountains as defensible borders and with the hills as the fertile land of settlement anchored the sacred mountain as a symbol of divine presence, security, and peace. In the second case, the widely scattered Jewish diaspora made the perception of Jerusalem as the mother city and earth navel reasonable. Although in both cases motifs were "borrowed" from the dominant cultures of which Israel was part, those motifs clustered about a symbol which gave form to concrete Jewish experience.

---

[25] Before long, however, Rome became an omphalos for the Christian West and Jerusalem became a pilgrimage center as well. These later developments deserve independent treatment.

[26] W. D. Davies, *The Gospel and the Land*, p. 367.

To impose a comparative category such as "sacred mountain" on a tradition is to risk turning up not so sacred molehills. Geographical symbolism is tied, at least in part, to geophysical reality. If particular manifestations of universal symbol structures indeed exist, they flower under the pressure of historical circumstances. As tantalizing as comparative generalizations may be, they must be tested against the explicit self-understanding to which the concrete data testify.

Finally, the intermediate position of rabbinic Judaism between wholly locative Samaritanism and wholly diasporic Christianity bears further study.[27] The Samaritans had their sacred mountain, the Christians had no earthly city, but the Jews had a mountain-city-center to which they were attached but which they may never have seen. Jerusalem was simultaneously reality and symbol. The heavenly Jerusalem never eclipsed the earthly in Jewish thought, yet the often sorry state of the real city encouraged the longing for the new Jerusalem.

This paradox, in the last analysis, rests on a fundamental principle of Jewish thought that develops over the period we have considered: the holiness of place is never absolute. In the pre-monarchial period the presence of Yahweh moved with the ark, sealing victories and defining the borders. No one shrine had a monopoly on the sacred. During the monarchy the Jerusalem establishment settled Yahweh in a house and gradually claimed such a monopoly, yet the prophetic tradition challenged the absolute trust vested in the sacred center. Even Solomon in his temple dedication speech, according to the Deuteronomist, recognizes that "heaven and the highest heaven cannot contain thee; how much less this house which I have built" (1 Kings 8:27). When Jerusalem was destroyed by the Babylonians, the paradoxical attitude toward the holy place was manifested in the differing responses of the survivors. On the one hand, men from the north came to worship Yahweh on the ruins of the temple (Jer. 41:4f.), testifying to the belief in the ongoing sanctity of the site. On the other hand, exiles in Babylon saw Yahweh to be a *miqdāš mě'at*, "little sanctuary" (Ezek. 11:16), wherever they were in exile. Yahweh had been liberated from the sacred place with which he had been identified. When the second temple fell, the rabbis debated whether or not the Shekhinah had fled with the flames into heaven and forsaken them but decided, rather, that the presence of God had accompanied them into exile (*Mekilta* 1:114f.). Jerusalem remained the ambiguous center, partaking of but not wholly containing the holiness of Yahweh. The center for Judaism was sacred but not ultimate.

---

[27] I borrow the contrast between "locative" and "diasporic" from Jonathan Z. Smith, "The Wobbling Pivot," *The Journal of Religion* 52 (1972): 146–49.